*Law*Basics

EVIDENCE

AUSTRALIA
Law Book Co.
Sydney

CANADA and USA
Carswell
Toronto

HONG KONG
Sweet & Maxwell Asia

NEW ZEALAND
Brookers
Wellington

SINGAPORE and MALAYSIA
Sweet & Maxwell Asia
Singapore and Kuala Lumpur

*Law*Basics

EVIDENCE

2nd Edition

by

Derek P. Auchie, LL.B. (Hons.), Dip.L.P.

Lecturer in Law, The Robert Gordon University, Aberdeen
Solicitor

THOMSON

TM

W. GREEN

First published 1998
Published in 2005 by W. Green & Son Ltd
21 Alva Street
Edinburgh EH2 4PS

Printed in Great Britain by Athenaeum Press,
Gateshead, Tyne & Wear

No natural forests were destroyed to make this product;
Only farmed timber was used and replanted

A CIP catalogue record for this book is available from the British Library

ISBN 0414015819

For my late grandfather

CONTENTS

CONTENTS

TABLE OF CASES

ABBREVIATIONS

"Dickson"	Dickson, *Evidence* (3rd ed., T&T Clark, 1887).
"ECHR"	European Convention on Human Rights as enacted by the Human Rights Act 1998.
"Harper and Hamilton"	Harper and Hamilton, *A Fingertip Guide to Criminal Law* (4th ed., Butterworths, 1999).
"Raitt"	F. Raitt, *Evidence* (3rd ed., W. Green/Sweet and Maxwell, 2001).
"Sheldon"	D. Sheldon, *Evidence, Cases and Materials* (2nd ed., W. Green/Sweet and Maxwell, 2002).
"the 1995 Act"	The Criminal Procedure (Scotland) Act 1995, c.46.
"Walker and Walker"	M. Ross, *Walker and Walker, The Law of Evidence in Scotland* (2nd ed., T&T Clark, 2000).
"Wilkinson"	A.B. Wilkinson, *The Scottish Law of Evidence* (The Law Society of Scotland, Butterworths, 1986).

PART 1. INTRODUCTION AND CONCEPTS

INTRODUCTION

Students will usually have only a vague idea about the content of an evidence module before embarking on it. It is unlike any other subject taught at undergraduate level in that it spans all other legal subject matter; it is genuinely generic in nature.

It is also highly practical. The subject is really about what happens (or should happen) in a court room. Cases involving the law of evidence, particularly criminal cases, arise every week in the appeal courts. Unlike any other legal topic, cases do not mark the extreme boundaries of the subject, so that a litigation only arises occasionally when the law at the fringes needs to be clarified. The law of evidence is pronounced upon week in week out at appeal level because it touches every case and is always evolving.

The law of evidence can also be highly controversial. Issues such as technicalities in search procedure, the questioning of a rape victim as to her sexual history with the accused (and possibly with others), the legitimate boundaries of police questioning methods, the use of expert evidence and the legality of police entrapment techniques are just some of the issues being grappled with regularly by the Scottish courts.

The law of evidence is not an easy subject to grasp or master. However, given the generic, highly practical, ever evolving and controversial nature of the subject, students should enjoy the experience. It is hoped that this book will assist with the process.

CONCEPTS

Types of evidence
It is, at a basic level, possible to categorise evidence according to type. There are five main types of evidence:

- Real evidence—a "thing" which is not a document, *e.g.* a bag of heroin in a drugs case.
- Documentary evidence—*e.g.* a contract in a breach of contract case or a receipt in a debt case. Other examples include a map, plan or diagram.
- Oral evidence—testimony in court from a witness.
- Affidavit evidence—this is a substitute for oral evidence and is a sworn statement, and is usually used where a witness cannot

attend personally or in an undefended divorce or child contact case, where evidence must be led.

- Agreed evidence—this can be any of the above agreed by the parties to avoid having to prove uncontroversial facts. The usual device is a joint minute signed by the parties and setting out the content of the agreed evidence.

The law of evidence has rules for the leading of all of these types of evidence which differ according to whether the case is criminal or civil and according to the nature of the case.

Burden of proof

The burden of proof is a device that deals with the following question: *which party* must prove the case? The standard of proof deals with the following question: *to what extent* must that party prove the case?

Three types of burden exist:

1. The persuasive burden. This is the most important form of burden, and it is attached to a particular party by law and never moves. Where a particular party requires to satisfy the court on a particular issue (bears the burden of proof on that issue) in order to succeed in the case, that party bears the persuasive burden on that issue.
2. The evidential burden. This is the burden on a party of producing sufficient evidence (often minimal) of a fact in order to allow the court to begin considering it. Sometimes the persuasive and evidential burdens fall on different parties. Where this happens, one party has to produce some evidence of the fact (evidential burden) and once this happens the other party must persuade the court that the fact is established (persuasive burden).
3. The tactical burden. This is not really a formal type of burden, but it is a device that allows the practical application of burdens to be understood. The tactical burden is the only one that *shifts* during the course of a case. The way in which the evidence is presented in court does not allow the easy identification of the allocation of burdens. The tactical burden mirrors the changing dynamics of a case.

When we deal with burdens in criminal and civil cases, we will see the operation of the persuasive and evidential burdens in action. While those burdens apply in civil as well as criminal cases, they play a more important role in criminal cases.

Why are burdens necessary? The main reason is to ensure that in any particular case, there will be a winner. In most cases, the court will be in no doubt as to which party has made out his case. However, sometimes, the case may be evenly balanced. In such a situation, the court can rely on the burden of proof to decide the case—it tilts the scales in one direction or the other in difficult cases. It is also useful in ensuring that the parties are aware of the points on which they must lead convincing evidence. Were it not for the burden of proof, the parties would not know which facts to concentrate on when preparing their case. So, for example a defender knows that he does not require to disprove an issue essential to his opponent's case. A pursuer will be aware that he does not require to counter his opponent's defence in order to win the case—it is for his opponent to establish it.

Standard of proof

This device tells the bearer of a burden *how* to prove his essential facts in order to discharge his burden of proof. In other words, it tells him to which standard his essential facts must be established. In civil cases, the standard of proof is "on the balance of probabilities" and in criminal cases, the standard is "beyond reasonable doubt".

Presumptions

Presumptions allow certain facts to be established by implication. A presumption has been defined as "an inference as to the existence of one fact, drawn from the existence of another fact" (*Dickson*, para.109).

So, an initial fact(s) must be established and this will allow the inference to be made.

There are two ways in which presumptions can be categorised:

- law or fact; and
- rebuttable or irrebuttable.

However there are only three types of presumption:

- irrebuttable presumptions of law;
- rebuttable presumptions of law;
- rebuttable presumptions of fact.

We will deal later with some specific examples both in criminal and civil cases.

Admissibility

Evidence can be relevant but it must still be admissible in order to be allowed to be produced in court. If not, it will be inadmissible and the court will not hear it or at least will refuse to consider it.

Some examples of inadmissible evidence are:

- secondary hearsay evidence in a criminal case;
- opinion evidence from a non-expert;

- evidence involuntarily extracted, *e.g.* a confession to a crime following violence by police officers;
- evidence recovered as a result of an illegally or unfairly conducted search in a criminal case.

Admissibility rules in criminal cases are normally motivated by a concern that the accused is not being treated fairly. In civil cases, the concern is usually of fairness between the parties. If the court is not persuaded that the evidence should be admitted, then the court will refuse to hear it. Sometimes, the court will have to hear the evidence in order to decide whether or not it should be admitted. In civil cases, this will be done by the court hearing the case and then deciding whether or not to exclude the evidence in question. In criminal cases, the same process usually occurs in the context of a special procedure known as a "trial within a trial" which is essentially a ring-fenced trial on the admissibility point only, separate from the trial at large.

Weight

The court will place a certain amount of weight on each piece of relevant and admissible evidence.

In criminal cases where there is a jury this will be a matter purely for the jury. The court (whether jury or judge), in concluding on each fact and in turn on the case, may disregard a piece of evidence (*e.g.* the testimony of a witness) or may place little or a lot of weight on it.

Sufficiency

This is a question of law—has a party with a burden adduced sufficient evidence in law to discharge the burden?

In a criminal case the defence could attack the sufficiency of the Crown case before the case is at an end, immediately after the end of the Crown case, by a motion of no case to answer.

Sufficiency is relevant to all cases, criminal and civil, and is concerned with the attainment by a party with a burden of proof of a certain minimum level of proof. It is different, however, from failing to meet the standard of proof.

Evidence and Human Rights

The Human Rights Act 1998 has had, and continues to have, a significant impact on the law of evidence, particularly in criminal cases. Where there is an actual or potential human rights point, this is raised at the relevant point in this book. By far the main impact has come from Articles 6 (fair trial) and 8 (privacy) of the ECHR. It is clear that this impact will only continue, and in many criminal appeals against conviction, there will be a domestic Scots law argument that will be run alongside a separate human rights argument.

PART 2. THE GENERAL PART

In this section, we deal with rules of evidence that are similar in both criminal and civil cases.

JUDICIAL KNOWLEDGE

Not every fact that a party relies upon in his case must be proven by leading evidence. Certain facts are so notorious or able to be immediately ascertained that it would be pointless adducing evidence of them. In England this concept is known as "judicial notice" and in Scotland, it is called "judicial knowledge". In both jurisdictions, however, the law is the same, therefore cases from England, as well as Scotland, are relevant here.

Notorious facts

These are facts that will not require to be proven, simply because no one would seriously dispute them, and to require that they be established by evidence would be both absurd and time-consuming. This category is extremely wide and can hardly be quantified. A few examples will suffice; the fact that night follows day; that a car is a mechanically propelled vehicle and that a pushbike is not; that two weeks is too short for human gestation—*Luffe* (1807); that cats are normally kept for domestic purposes—*Nye v Niblett* (1918).

There are some less obvious examples of notorious facts. For example, *Taylor v Glasgow Corporation* (1921) was a damages action following the death of a child who ate poisonous berries. It was held by the House of Lords to be within judicial knowledge that children are prone to be drawn to and tempted to eat colourful berries whenever they can be reached. The fact of such a temptation on the part of children generally, was notorious and so was within judicial knowledge.

In *Doyle v Ruxton* (1999) for the purposes of a liquor licensing prosecution, the High Court held that drinks with certain well known brand names—such as McEwen's Export, Guinness, Carlsberg Special Brew and Holsten Pils lager—are all alcoholic drinks. This fact was deemed to be within judicial knowledge. The fact that pension funds had recently, at the time of the hearing, been falling in value, was been held to be a fact that is not within judicial knowledge—evidence in this area would be required (*Kennedy v Kennedy* (2004)).

Judicial Notice after Inquiry

These cases are more difficult and involve the court claiming that a fact is within judicial knowledge since it has been verified by the court after checking with a reliable source. An example is the definition of a word contained in a dictionary—such a definition can be regarded as being within judicial knowledge (see *Inland Revenue Commissioners v Russell* (1955), where the word "stepchild" in a tax statute was interpreted by the House of Lords with reference to the dictionary meaning of that word). Another example might be a map or a historical reference work. However, not all reference works fall within this category.

For example, in the Outer House case of *Cavin v Kinnaird* (1994), it was held that the stopping distances in the Highway Code could not replace the leading of evidence. However, such data could be used to "check evidence given in court". More recently, the Inner House has stated, in the context of a medical negligence action, that the content of medical textbooks, no matter how authoritative, is not within judicial knowledge, and such content would only obtain any evidential value if put to a medical witness to be commented upon—*Gerrard v Royal Infirmary of Edinburgh* (2005).

In *Kennedy v Smith & Ansvar Insurance Co Ltd* (1976), Lord McDonald in the Outer House had regard, in an insurance dispute arising out of a road traffic accident, to evidence suggesting that the driver was unaccustomed to drinking alcohol and that he had taken alcohol on an empty stomach. These factors were treated by the court as adminicles of evidence that supported an inference that the accident had been caused by the driver having been under the influence of alcohol. The Inner House, in overturning the original decision, held that such matters were not within judicial knowledge and that medical evidence on the effect of alcohol in these circumstances should have been led.

The content of the law

The content of Scots law, from whatever source, is regarded as being within judicial knowledge. Foreign law is not and has to be proven as if it were a fact. For these purposes, English law is regarded as foreign law. This does not mean, for example, that English case law must be ignored by the Scottish courts. Where Scots and English law are the same, English case law will be within judicial knowledge. However, where the issue before the court is the content of English law, and where Scots law is distinct in the area, the content of English law will require to be proven as a fact.

Judicial knowledge of Scots law extends to relevant Acts of Parliament, case law, Acts of Sederunt and Adjournal and applicable EU law. There is some doubt surrounding the status of Statutory Instruments, but according to *Walker and Walker* (para.19.19.2) and *Raitt* (para.4.05-4.06), at least in criminal cases, these fall to be judicially noted (*Herkes v Dickie* (1958)). Other government orders, not listed above, are not regarded as being within judicial knowledge (*Herkes v Dickie* (1958); *Donnelly v Carmichael* (1996)).

It seems possible that the content of Scots law could be regarded as within judicial knowledge as a result of the notorious nature of the law. This was the basis of the decision in *Valentine v Macphail* (1986), where a bench of five judges in the High Court held that the fact that a camic breathalyser machine was an approved device for the purposes of the road traffic legislation (such machines had to be approved by government order, not normally a part of Scots law falling within judicial knowledge) was within judicial knowledge as a fact that had been ascertained by the sheriff from earlier cases where the order had been produced (in this case it had not). Such uses of notoriety on the content of the law will, however, be rare.

Personal knowledge
Sometimes a judge will attempt to use his own personal knowledge to infer that a fact is established. This is not an example of judicial knowledge. The judge must clear his mind of all personal knowledge and decide the case only on the evidence presented. This applies even in arbitration where the arbitrator will normally possess some expertise on the issue in question. For example, in *Dyer v Wilsons and Clyde Coal Co* (1915), the arbitrator's decision was overturned on appeal by the Inner House where it was held that evidence of a claim should not have been refused by the arbitrator by relying upon his own knowledge of the local work market. The same decision would have been reached had the case been before a public court as opposed to an arbitrator.

Similarly, where a judge effectively conducts his own examination of the evidence and then uses it in the decision making process, the decision will be vulnerable to appeal. So, in *Hattie v Leitch* (1889), where the sheriff examined the locus after the evidence was over, in order to test the accuracy of an account of events given by certain witnesses, he was held to have gathered his own evidence and so his decision was overturned on appeal.

In *Aitken v Wood* (1921), the justices examined the bruised arm of the complainer while deliberating outwith the presence of the parties. The High Court held that this was a fatal irregularity, in circumstances where the complainer had not shown her arm during the course of her evidence. The examination constituted the taking of evidence by the court. However, a visit by a juror to the locus, when he was there legitimately in connection with his employment, was held to be distinguishable from that situation (*Gray v HMA* (2005)).

OPINION EVIDENCE

There are two types evidence led in court:

1. Evidence as to fact.

2.   Opinion evidence.

Generally speaking, any witness can (as long as he is a competent witness and the evidence is admissible (see later on both)) give evidence as to fact. However, only skilled witnesses can give opinion evidence. Some common examples of such evidence are:

- a medical consultant in a personal injury case;
- a computer expert in a case alleging the downloading of unlawful pornographic material;
- a valuer in a dispute about what something is worth, *e.g.* shares, a pension, a matrimonial home, a car (surveyor, financial adviser, accountant);
- a safety expert on the state of a piece of equipment or premises;
- a technical expert on the workings of a piece of machinery or structure;
- a drugs expert on whether a quantity of drugs is for personal use or onward supply (usually a drugs force police officer—see below).

Sometimes reference is made to an "expert" witness, however, the better terminology, and the one adopted by *Walker and Walker* is "skilled witness". A skilled witness need not be regarded as an expert in his field. For example, the drugs force police officer mentioned at the end of the above list will be regarded as a skilled witness, but not necessarily an expert. The same would apply to, *e.g.* a social worker giving evidence of his opinion on whether a child has formed a bond with foster carers. However, these two terms are, for convenience, used interchangeably here.

The rule then is that only skilled witnesses can give opinion evidence. However, we need to consider in more detail some of the aspects of this important form of evidence.

The role of opinion evidence

The main Scottish case on the role of the skilled witness is *Davie v Magistrates of Edinburgh* (1953). In that case, Lord President Cooper stated at p.40:

> "Expert witnesses, however skilled or eminent, can give no more than evidence. They cannot usurp the functions of the jury or Judge…Their duty is to furnish the Judge or jury with the necessary scientific criteria for testing the accuracy of their conclusions, so as to enable the Judge or jury to form their own independent judgement by the application of these criteria to the facts proved in evidence. The scientific opinion evidence, if intelligible, convincing and tested, becomes a factor (and often an important factor) for consideration

along with the whole other evidence in the case, but the decision is for the Judge or jury."

As a consequence of this rule, it has been made clear in Scotland that an expert cannot give evidence on an issue that the court is required to determine. So, *e.g.* in *Galletly v Laird* (1953), expert evidence on the question of whether the content of certain books was indecent or obscene was disallowed. The basis for this was that this question was the very one the court had to answer in considering the criminal charge before it, so a witness could not usurp that function, even an expert one. Also, in *Ingram v Macari (No.2)* (1983), the accused was acquitted on a charge of shamelessly indecent conduct (selling certain magazines of a pornographic nature in his shop). The High Court reversed the acquittal and referred the case back to the sheriff to proceed. The sheriff had admitted the evidence of a psychologist and a psychiatrist, who had made special studies of pornography, and who gave evidence on the question of whether the magazines were "liable to deprave and corrupt the morals of the lieges". However, the High Court held that this question was the very one with which the court was concerned and was a question of law, not one that could be resolved by opinion evidence. The opinion evidence had, in this case, been wrongly admitted.

A skilled witness holds no special status *per se*. Such a witness cannot usurp the role of the court and his evidence must be weighed along with all other evidence in the decision making process.

A natural consequence of this is that in a case involving conflicting expert evidence, the judge or jury is not obliged to simply choose between the views expressed. The court may ignore all expert evidence tendered and adopt a different view, as long as the view taken is based on other evidence which is accepted, and not on the court's own assumptions.

Who may qualify as a skilled witness?
In order to qualify as a skilled witness, a person is not required to have a certain minimum level of qualifications or experience. So, *e.g.* an amateur handwriting "expert" was accepted as an opinion witness in *R v Silverlock* (1894). This was further demonstrated in the case of *Hewart v Edinburgh Corporation* (1944), where the Inner House held that the question of whether a hole in a public road could be said to be dangerous was one that could be addressed by a police constable, part of whose duty was to report such dangers. So, as long as the witness can be shown to possess some experience or has informally acquired expertise in the field, the evidence is likely to be admissible. In *White v. H.M. Advocate* (1986), experienced police officers were permitted to give evidence as to the amount of a drug which a user might possess for his own consumption (as opposed to for onward sale purposes). Again, in *Wilson v H.M. Advocate* (1988), police officers in the drugs squad were allowed to disclose the "received wisdom of persons concerned in drugs enforcement" garnered at seminars and in discussions with customs officers on the question of methods of

importation of cannabis resin. So, the important question is not whether the witness possesses certain qualifications, but what the knowledge and experience of the witness is.

Whether a witness is formally qualified or not, it is necessary to establish during the evidences that the witness is properly (and preferably well) qualified to give opinion evidences about the matter in hand. The first questions asked of a medical witness, *e.g.* will be about his studies, degrees, diplomas, research, publications, memberships of professional bodies and experience in the field concerned. It will usually be a simple matter to establish the witness's expertise, given the need for formal qualifications in most scientific or technical fields.

The importance of leading opinion evidence
Where evidence from a skilled witness is required but not led, this can be fatal, so it is very important to be in a position to judge when such evidence is required and when it is not. The absence of opinion evidence was fatal in the Inner House case of *Columbia Steam Navigation Co v Burns* (1895). The dispute in that case arose out of a collision between two ships. The court was asked to draw certain inferences about the cause of the accident from the nature and extent of damage to one of the vessels. It was held that skilled evidence on the nature and extent of the damage was needed and the inference requested could not be made without it.

Establishing the factual basis for opinion evidence
Before opinion evidence can competently be led, a factual basis for the expression of such opinions must be established. Thus, in *Blagojevic v H.M. Advocate* (1995), a case in which the accused disputed the reliability of his confession, expert psychological evidence as to the accused's "suggestibility" was excluded. This was on the technical ground that, since the accused had not himself given evidence as to the nature of his interrogation, there was no proper evidential foundation for opinion evidence regarding the stress or pressure to which the accused had been subjected in police interviews. Therefore, the factual evidence must come first, followed by the opinion evidence based on those facts. See also *McD v HMA* (2002).

Exception to the rule: opinion evidence from lay witnesses
In some situations, it is possible for a non-skilled witness to provide opinion evidence. However, the scope for such a possibility is narrow. The exception only applies where the witness is able to comment on something that he or she has seen, heard or sensed and where it would be reasonable for a lay person to offer an opinion on such a matter. For example, in *Kenny v Tudhope* (1984), police officers were permitted to give evidence that the accused's breath smelled of alcohol, his speech was slurred and his eyes glazed, where the charge was one of driving while unfit to do so through the use of drink or drugs. It can be seen, however,

that in this example the issue is one upon which most adults could be expected to form a reasonably reliable view, given an awareness of the everyday use and abuse of alcohol and its effects. The same cannot be said for less commonplace occurrences and conditions, and whether expert evidence is required is ultimately a matter of law. Other examples include:

- identification of an individual, notably the accused in the dock. This is an expression of opinion where the person in the dock is said to be the same person as the one seen at the locus of a crime;
- identification of handwriting of a spouse or friend;
- opinion as to whether a vehicle was travelling fast (but not whether it was travelling over the speed limit; a skilled witness would be needed for this).

Credibility and reliability of a witness

Although the court must ultimately decide on the issue of whether any witness is credible and reliable, the High Court has recently held that expert evidence on such matters is competent. This view was adopted in the important case of *Campbell v HMA* (2004). This was a case arising out of the notorious "ice cream" wars fought in Glasgow in the 1980s. There were three appellants in this case, Campbell, Steele and Gray. For present purposes, we are concerned with a particular and common aspect of the arguments on behalf of Campbell and Steele.

This case resulted from a referral to the High Court from the Scottish Criminal Cases Review Commission of the 1984 convictions of Campbell and Steele for *inter alia* murder by setting fire to the door of the house occupied by the victims. One important source of evidence against the accused was the evidence of a number of police officers who had claimed that they had noted certain incriminating statements from both accused word for word. The appellants produced new evidence in the form of expert reports and testimony from two expert witnesses. Both experts concluded that it was highly unlikely that, in either case, all of the officers could have noted the statements made by the accused in virtually identical terms, as was claimed by the officers, unless there had been some form of collusion between them on the content of their notebooks in this regard (which was denied by them). This evidence was said to be based upon experiments conducted by the experts as well as on their qualifications, experience and scientific literature.

Although the High Court refused to take into account the findings of the experts on the question of the reliability of the police officers' accounts (it was held that such an assessment was a matter for the court, not an expert witness) it allowed the appeal and quashed the convictions on the basis that the original convictions were unsafe.

This decision is a landmark one in that the court accepts that expert evidence involving an examination of human behaviour or propensity that may have an indirect bearing on reliability or credibility can be admissible. The commentator to the SCCR report of the case, Sir Gerald Gordon, puts it in this way:

> "..although it is still the law that evidence as to the reliability or credibility of a particular witness is inadmissible, being a question for the jury, it is competent to lead expert evidence bearing on the likelihood that evidence of the kind given, or in the circumstances to which it relates, is credible or reliable."

To put it another way, while an expert cannot give direct evidence in which he says "I think this witness has lied or is an unreliable witness" since this is purely within the domain of the court to decide, an expert can give evidence that is designed indirectly to cast doubt on the credibility or reliability of the account of a witness.

The *Campbell* case has further implications than this and has been cited on a number of occasions since (see below).

Expert psychological evidence led on the issue of the common pattern of disclosure by a complainer in cases of child sexual abuse was declared inadmissible by Lord Osborne at first instance in *HMA v Grimmond* (2001). It seems that if such evidence were presented in a post-*Campbell* case, the evidence itself (dealing with research on the pattern of a partial disclosure followed later by a full disclosure in child sexual abuse cases) would be admissible, although not any conclusions reached by the expert to the effect that the witnesses accounts were credible and reliable.

In fact, the *Campbell* case has far wider implications. Expert evidence of all shapes and sizes may now be able to be led where such evidence might have a bearing on the likelihood of other evidence given being credible or reliable. In particular, all kinds of psychological, behavioural and personality evidence will now be admissible, as well as evidence (such as in the *Campbell* case) that tests on a scientific basis the likelihood of something having occurred as claimed, such as something claimed to have been said, heard, seen or sensed.

Suggestibility of the interviewee or suspect

Expert psychological or psychiatric evidence can be led in order to argue that the terms of an interview (notably a police interview) cannot be relied upon and is, therefore, inadmissible (see "admissibility"). The authorities were split on this issue until the landmark decision of *Campbell*, above. This is because in *Campbell*, the High Court suggests that any evidence that might cast doubt on the credibility or reliability of a witness account is admissible. This question was not decided in *Blagogevic v HMA* (1995), since the evidence was refused admission for a different reason, but it now seems beyond doubt that such evidence is admissible. Indeed, evidence of similar types seems to be admissible, as will be seen from the examples below.

Furthermore, since *Campbell*, the High Court has commented in the following general terms:

> "Expert evidence may be given, by a suitably qualified person and by reference to a recognised body of expert knowledge, as to the existence in a witness of a medical, psychiatric or psychological condition which could account for the witness giving an untrue account....No doubt at least one reason why such evidence is admissible is that it relates to matters which a jury do not have the opportunity to investigate or the expertise to diagnose." (*Mackay v HMA* (2004)).

This would also cover a suggestible interviewee.

Low intelligence

A similar but distinct question is whether expert evidence on the low intelligence of an interviewee or suspect can be led, with a view to having evidence declared inadmissible. Such expert evidence is probably admissible when one takes into account the quotation (above) from the *Mackay* case. More specifically, in *LB v HMA* (2003), evidence was presented from a psychiatrist as to the appellant's verbal IQ and his ability to understand a caution. A clinical psychologist also gave evidence about research showing that persons of a similar age and ability to the appellant were unable to understand the common law caution (see pages 63–64 later on this caution). The appeal was not concerned with the admissibility question, but there seems to have been no concern in the appeal court about the admission of this evidence by the trial judge.

Predisposition to lying

Such evidence is a little more problematic. In *Mackay v HMA* (2004), the issue was the admissibility of certain evidence under ss.274–275 of the 1995 Act (dealing with sexual history evidence—see later at pages 35–37) concerning the tendency of the complainer (a school-age child) to exaggerate and tell lies as evidenced by previous behaviour. Evidence was intended to be led from teachers and the head teacher. In upholding the refusal of the application to lead the evidence the court commented that there was no underlying psychiatric or psychological condition affecting the pupil (see the above quotation).

On the other hand, Lord Justice-Clerk Gill in *McBrearty v HMA* (2004), comments (the point having been conceded by the Crown), that certain evidence from a psychiatrist obtained post-trial would have been admissible had it been presented. The evidence here would have been to the effect that the complainer had a *pathological* predisposition to lie. These observations are commented upon with approval in the *Mackay* case, above.

Empirical expert evidence
The *Campbell* case has implications even beyond those discussed above. Another new aspect emerges from this case. Professor Clifford (one of the defence expert witnesses) carried out no fewer than four empirical studies (experiments) in which he tested, through the use of simulated memory situations, the likelihood of the incriminating statements being recalled in the circumstances claimed. These trials led him to the conclusion that in the case of Campbell, the chances of any random four, or even two officers recalling a sentence of 24 words (the number of words in the alleged incriminating statement made by Campbell) in identical terms, without some collaboration between them, was 'infinitesimal'. A similar, if less pronounced conclusion was reached in relation to the memory recall of the shorter statement of Steele. These were, then, tailor-made experiments, designed to test the scientific theory behind the evidence. The court embraced these tests, and again, this opens the possibility of similar empirical evidence-gathering in any other suitable case, whether or not credibility and/or reliability is being challenged.

PART 3. THE LAW OF EVIDENCE IN CRIMINAL CASES

BURDEN OF PROOF

The general rule is that the evidential and persuasive burdens (see Part 1 on these) in a criminal case fall squarely on the Crown. It has been made clear that this is a natural consequence of the presumption of innocence (see the comments to this effect by Lord Justice Clerk *Thomson in McKenzie v HMA* (1959)). It is crucial that the burden of proof and the consequences of that burden are properly explained to the jury, otherwise there will be a misdirection (see the guidance given by the High Court in *Lyttle v HMA* (2004)).

However, there are certain exceptions to this general rule.

Special defences
An accused person who seeks to establish either of the special defences of insanity or diminished responsibility bears the evidential and persuasive burdens (*HMA v Mitchell* (1951)—insanity; *Carraher v HMA* (1946)—diminished responsibility).

Where one of the other special defences is pled (alibi, self-defence or incrimination) the evidential burden is on the accused, but the persuasive burden remains with the Crown (*Lambie v HMA* (1973)). As explained earlier in Part 1 on burdens, this means that the accused has to initially adduce some evidence of the special defence and the Crown then requires to establish that the defence does not apply. This may seem odd and in practice the accused will, of course, do all he can to establish the defence. However, in an evenly balanced case (cases where a burden does actually make a difference) the fact that the persuasive burden remains with the Crown will mean that the accused will be given the benefit of any doubt. It is clear that the jury must be directed properly on this "splitting" of the burden (*Gilmour v HMA* (1989)).

Statutory exceptions

Various statutory exceptions exist. These consist mainly of offences to which there is a statutory defence of reasonable excuse or justification. In such cases the onus often shifts to the accused, for example:

- s.4(3) and 5(2) of the Road Traffic Act 1988—defence of no likelihood of driving;
- s.48 of the Criminal Law Consolidation (Scotland) Act 1995— reasonable excuse defence for possession of offensive weapon in public place.

Although there is some doubt on this, it seems that in such cases the accused bears both the evidential and persuasive burdens (*Grieve v MacLeod* (1967)).

The reversal of the burden of proof in a statutory provision can, in some cases, lead to the legislation being in conflict with the provisions of the ECHR, more specifically Article 6(2), in which the presumption of innocence is enshrined. See, as examples of challenges of this kind, *R v Lambert* (2001), and *McIntosh, Petitioner* (2001).

Facts peculiarly within the knowledge of the accused

In some cases where there are facts peculiarly within the knowledge of the accused, the law will require at least a *prima facie* case from the Crown, after which the persuasive burden of proof shifts to the accused. It is often said in such cases that there arises a "presumption of guilt" which the accused must successfully counter.

The main example of this is the doctrine of recent possession of stolen goods. The leading case is *Fox v Patterson* (1948). In that case, involving a charge of theft of some metal alloy, Lord Justice-General Cooper set out the conditions that apply in such cases:

> "If the rule is to have full effect in shifting the onus from the prosecution to the accused and raising a presumption of guilt which the accused must redargue or fail, three conditions must concur: (a) that the stolen goods should be found in the possession of the accused; (b) that the interval between the theft of the goods and their discovery in the accused's possession should be short...... and (c) that

there should be 'other criminative circumstances' over and above the bare fact of possession."

This doctrine was applied by the High Court in the case *Cassidy v McLeod* (1981). The accused were charged with and convicted of theft by housebreaking of bottles and cans of beer and cider and some crates. The day after the break-in, they were found in possession of odd quantities of cans and bottles of alcohol, some of which corresponded to the quantities and brands of drinks stolen. They were also in possession of some of the stolen crates. There was a trail of crates, bottles and cans leading from the scene of the crime which petered out in some waste ground, heading in the general direction of the place where the goods were found. All three conditions for the application of the doctrine were held to be established. On the question of "other criminative circumstances" the court pointed to the odd numbers of alcoholic drinks, their correspondence with the ones stolen, the presence of some of the stolen crates and the trail of items leading from the scene.

STANDARD OF PROOF

The standard of proof in criminal cases is proof "beyond reasonable doubt". The interaction of the burden and standard of proof in criminal cases means that the Crown must establish the guilt of the accused beyond reasonable doubt.

What does "beyond reasonable doubt" mean? The Scottish courts are reluctant to tell us the answer to this seemingly simple question. However, the case law on directions to juries on this has led to the High Court approving the following definition:

- Where the evidence raises a reasonable doubt in the mind of the juror or judge as to the guilt of the accused, the standard has not been attained.

So, what does "reasonable doubt" mean? The High Court has defined this also:

- A reasonable doubt arises if it is a doubt that would cause the juror or judge to hesitate or pause in the conduct of his own affairs before taking a decision.

It has been made clear that even the slightest deviation from this definition of "reasonable doubt" in a jury direction may well be fatal to a conviction. In *MacDonald v HMA* (1996), it was held that the sheriff had misdirected the jury when he defined a reasonable doubt as one that would cause the jurors, in the conduct of their own affairs, to *stop* doing something. It was held that by referring to *stopping* doing something as opposed to *hesitating or pausing* before doing it, the sheriff had misdirected the jury on the standard of proof by overstating it. The appeal was allowed and the conviction quashed.

In *Buchanan v HMA* (1998), the sheriff again overstated the definition of reasonable doubt, this time by referring to it as a doubt that would *dissuade* the juror from a course of action. This, it was held, was different from a doubt that would cause the juror to *hesitate or pause*. Once again, the appeal was allowed, but this time a retrial was authorised.

It has been held that to refer to the standard as one where the jury had to be "reasonably sure" is a misdirection (*A v HMA* (2003)). However, in that case the appeal was refused. The trial judge had mentioned "beyond reasonable doubt" as well as being "reasonably sure" during his direction. The High Court held that the overall impact of the direction taken as a whole was that no miscarriage of justice had occurred.

The courts have made it clear that deviation from the standard direction, while permissible, is usually unwise—see the comments of Lord Justice Clerk Thomson in *Mackenzie v HMA* (1959), approved in *A v HMA* (2003). In the latter case, Lord Justice-Clerk Gill, in delivering the unanimous opinion of the court, put it in this way:

> "...a restatement of a recognised direction in other terms may complicate or modify the legal test and in that way create the risk of a misdirection."

However, the fact that the standard direction is not *mandatory* has been made clear by the High Court (*Meyl v HMA* (2005)).

SUFFICIENCY

The Crown must lead sufficient evidence in order to secure a conviction in a criminal case. There are two aspects to consider on the subject of sufficiency:

1. Proof of the crucial facts (*facta probanda*) of the crime libelled.
2. Proof of such facts by corroborated evidence.

We will deal with each in turn.

Crucial facts of a crime

The "*facta probanda*" (crucial facts; literal translation—"facts to be proved") in any criminal charge must be proven by corroborated evidence led by the Crown (*Smith v Lees* (1997)). If the Crown fails to do so, there is an insufficiency of evidence and the accused cannot be convicted of the crime libelled. Having stated the general rule, we must now break it down.

Facta probanda (crucial facts)
The crucial facts will vary from charge to charge. One way of explaining what the *facta probanda* are is to say that in every case, the Crown will

have to establish by corroborated evidence that (1) the crime libelled (the crime forming the charge on the complaint or indictment) was committed and (2) it was committed by the accused. We will now examine each of these.

That the crime was committed
Each crime has certain essential ingredients. Those ingredients come together to form a definition of the crime. In each case, the definition of a crime can be expressed in a sentence or two. Some concise yet accurate definitions of some of the main crimes are expressed in *Harper and Hamilton*. A good judicial example is that provided by Lord Justice-General Rodger in *Smith v Lees*, where he says (of the definition of rape that existed at that time (it has since been modified)):

> "..in rape...the Crown requires to prove (1) penetration of the complainer's vagina by (2) the accused's private member (3) forcibly, and (4) without the complainer's consent. These four fundamental facts require to be established by corroborated evidence."

So, in every rape case, these were the crucial facts that had to be established. Each crime has a different definition. Different facts will therefore require to be proven in the case of each different crime.

That it was committed by the accused
The identification of the accused as the perpetrator of the crime must be established in one of several recognised manners and the identification evidence must be of sufficient quality. We will now deal with these issues.

Methods of identification
There are various methods of identification that the Crown can resort to. The most common is a "dock identification" where the accused is pointed out by the witness as he is sitting in the dock. It has been made clear that where such a method of identification is chosen, the witness must physically point to the accused, and reference to "the accused" or to the accused by name, or both, will not suffice (*Bruce v HMA* (1936)). Where the witness is giving evidence from behind a screen (see later under vulnerable witnesses) then care must be taken to ensure that a positive identification of the accused takes place. In such a case, identification by reference to a name and description of relationship to the witness will be insufficient (*P v Williams* (2005)).

The second most common method of identification of an accused is by use of an identity parade, where the witness must pick out the offender from a line up of the accused and various volunteers. It has been held that where identification is in issue, good practice dictates that the Crown should hold an identity parade and not simply rely on a dock identification (*Holland v HMA* (2003)). The accused has a right to insist upon an identity parade being held in any case, under s.290 of the 1995 Act.

A third method of identifying the accused occurs where a witness has pointed out the accused to another witness at or near the scene of the crime, soon after the offence has been committed and where that other witness gives evidence in court that the accused (in the dock) was the person pointed out to them. This method of identification is used by the Crown when the witness who pointed out the accused at the time is then unable to positively identify the accused in the dock at the later trial. This form of identification was used and approved of by the High Court on appeal in *Muldoon v Herron* (1970). Similarly, where a witness has pointed out the accused during an identity parade, a witness who has observed that parade can later give evidence to the effect that the accused was pointed out. This can be done, again, where the original witness cannot positively identify the accused at the trial (*Bennett v HMA* (1976)).

It is also possible for the Crown to have the accused identified by photograph (*Howarth v HMA* (1992)). Similarly, where the witness does not see the accused, but hears his voice, he can be later identified in this way (*Burrows v HMA* (1951), in this case there was insufficient evidence, but in principle, the possibility of identification by voice was accepted). It is also possible to identify the accused by dental impressions (*Hay v HMA* (1968)), handwriting samples (*Campbell v Mackenzie* (1974)), and CCTV footage (*Bowie v Tudhope* (1986)).

Quality of identification evidence
Assuming that the Crown adopts a recognised method of identification of the accused, the question remains, how good does the identification require to be? The answer is that the identification need not be unequivocal, but must be positive. Where a witness gives evidence that the accused *resembles* the perpetrator of the crime, this is regarded as evidence of a positive identification, sufficient to corroborate an explicit identification (*Ralston v HMA* (1989); *Farmer v HMA* (1991)). Where the witness identifies the accused, and adds the words "I think" this may be treated as a positive identification (*Farmer v HMA* (1991)).

On the other hand, an identification attempt in which the witness stated that the accused "doesn't look unlike" the perpetrator, even where the witness elaborated by explaining that he was making this statement in connection with the build and facial appearance of the accused, was held to not constitute a positive identification of the accused (*MacDonald v HMA* (1998)).

Of course, each identification attempt will require to be viewed on its own facts and in the context of the other available evidence, so no hard and fast rules can be drawn in this area.

CORROBORATED EVIDENCE

(1) General
This is the second part of the subject of sufficiency and requires to be examined in some detail.

The basic rule
The corroboration rule requires, at its core, at least two pieces of evidence that are from independent sources. One piece of evidence will not be enough. One hundred pieces of evidence from one source will not be enough.

Not only must the two pieces of evidence be from independent sources, they must coincide. Where the two pieces of evidence conflict with each other, the corroboration rule is not satisfied. In what way, then, must they coincide? This question has taken up a significant amount of the High Court's time in the past. The law now seems settled following the five-judge decision in the landmark case of *Fox v HMA* (1998). The corroborating (supporting) evidence must "*confirm or support*" (these were the words used by the High Court in *Fox*) the other piece of evidence being relied upon. So, in most cases the courts will identify the main (strongest) source of evidence and will ask if the weaker source confirms or supports it. It should be noted that the court in *Fox* dispelled the notion that the corroborative evidence had to be more consistent with guilt than with innocence (*Mackie v HMA* (1995) was, therefore, disapproved). Therefore, an alternative innocent account of events by the accused will not rob the Crown evidence of its potentially corroborative value (*Chatam v HMA* (2005)).

Neutral evidence does not corroborate
Since the corroborating evidence must "confirm or support" the principal piece of evidence, neutral evidence can never corroborate, no matter how much of it there is.

In *Gallagher v HMA* (2000), the accused appealed against a conviction for robbery and assault to severe injury. The principal source of evidence was the testimony of the complainer. The complainer claimed that the accused and the co-accused were involved in the assault. The Crown relied upon three adminicles of evidence as corroboration; (1) the accused's admission of being in the flat at the time, (2) around a week after the incident blood was found on the accused's trainers, but there was no evidence to suggest that he had worn them on the day or that the blood belonged to the complainer, and (3) the accused was seen running away from the flat at the time of the incident. The High Court allowed the appeal and quashed the conviction, all three of these adminicles were regarded as being entirely neutral. The third, it was held, could be consistent with running away from the scene of a crime in which the accused did not wish to be implicated.

A further interesting, and borderline, case is *Gonshaw v Bamber (No.1)* (2004).

The question of whether a particular adminicle is neutral or incriminating when taken with the principal source, can often be a matter of context. An example that demonstrated this is the case of *Armit v O'Donnell* (1999), where a confession was held to be sufficiently corroborated by the presence of the accused near the scene shortly after the police were called. This case demonstrates that a single piece of evidence (not several, as was the case in both *Gallagher* and *Gonshaw*) can, in context, be sufficient to corroborate.

Inconsistent evidence
Where the evidence relied upon for corroboration does not match the principal evidence, it cannot be said to confirm or support it and will not be regarded as corroborative. In *Macdonald v Scott* (1993), the accused was convicted of assault. However, on appeal, the Crown conceded that there was not the necessary "conjunction of testimony" between the two sources of evidence relied upon at the trial. In this case the two sources consisted of eye witness accounts. One witness gave evidence that the accused punched the complainer while the complainer was still standing. The other witness spoke of the complainer being forced to the ground and being kicked and punched to the head and body. These accounts were clearly divergent, so they did not corroborate one another. A more obvious case of divergence occurred in *Miller v HMA* (1994), where one witness spoke of a stabbing in the toilet of a house and another spoke of a punch to the chest in the hallway (see also *TM v HMA* (2005)).

Partial corroboration
It is not unusual to find a charge that consists of a number of component parts. This is common, particularly in assault charges, but can happen in any charge. It is clear that the Crown does not have to corroborate each and every part of the libel (wording of the charge) as long as the main part of the charge can be corroborated. A good example of this is the case of *Campbell v Vannet* (1998). There, the charge was that the accused had punched the complainer on the face, caused her to fall to the ground, had seized hold of her and had swung her about, all to her injury. Only the punch was corroborated by two eye-witnesses, the rest of the libel was spoken to by only one witness. The High Court upheld the conviction on the whole charge, since the main part of the libel had been corroborated.

(2) Corroboration of a confession
A confession by an accused person is regarded as a very strong piece of evidence against him. This is because it is a statement by the accused against his own interests and is therefore regarded as less likely to be

fabricated. It should be made clear that the word "confession" is used in this book to refer to any incriminating statement made by the accused, and not only what is traditionally thought to be a confession, that is, a full account of the crime.

Of course, some confessions are extracted unfairly and we will return to this later. Assuming that the confession has been given freely and fairly, however, usually little will suffice to effectively corroborate it. It has been said, however, that much will depend upon the circumstances of the case and that it cannot be said as a rule that very little will be required in every case to corroborate a confession (*Meredith v Lees* (1992) per Lord Justice-General Hope). We have already dealt with the case of *Armit v O'Donnell*, above, and this offers a good example of minimal evidence operating to corroborate an explicit and clear confession.

Special knowledge confessions

Such confessions are sometimes said to be exceptions to the usual corroboration rule. A special knowledge confession is a confession that contains within it, information about how the crime was committed where the only *reasonable* explanation for the confessor having such information is that he was the perpetrator of the crime (*Woodland v Hamilton* (1990)). The idea is that such confessions, also known as "self-corroborating confessions", combine a confession of guilt with knowledge of the crime. Accordingly, although the evidence is coming from one source (the confessor) it represents two pieces of evidence—the confession of guilt, plus information about the crime. Such confessions are used routinely by the Crown and this is a very important device for obtaining a conviction in a case where there is no other evidence available. Of course, the special knowledge will have to be confirmed by another source, but this is not corroborative material. So, for example in a housebreaking case the householder will have to give evidence to confirm what was stolen, from where, and how the intruder gained entry. The idea is that this evidence should correspond with the details in the confession of the suspect.

This does not mean that the *only* explanation for the possession of such knowledge is that the confessor is the perpetrator of the crime. Indeed, the details of the crime might be publicly known by the time the confession is made. It was argued in *Wilson v HMA* (1987), since that information about the crime was in the public domain by the time of the confession, the special knowledge exhibited in the confession could not be regarded as sufficient to corroborate it. However, the High Court, in upholding the conviction for murder, held that the confessions were "redolent of having been made by someone who had been present when the crime was committed".

Sometimes a confession will contain information that is accurate and information that is not. Where this occurs, the court must disregard the inaccurate information in the confession and concentrate on the accurate information. The court should come to a view on whether, from this information alone, it can be said that the confession satisfies the *Woodland* test. In other words, the fact that an account contains inaccurate information as well as accurate, does not rob the confession of its self-corroborating status—see *Gilmour v HMA* (1982).

A confession can qualify as a special knowledge confession even if the information contained in it is minimal. There is no rule that a certain amount of accurate information is required. For example, the case of *MacDonald v HMA* (1988), where a short statement by the accused in which he revealed the identity of his accomplices and no more, was sufficient.

In the *Woodland* case itself, a different result occurred. There, the accused was found guilty of theft of a video recorder. The only evidence against the accused was a confession by him which referred to him having been in conversation with his co-accused and in which he named the resetter of the video. However, eleven months had passed between the date of the crime and the confession, and it was possible that the accused could have obtained the name of the resetter from the co-accused. In these circumstances, the confession did not qualify as a special knowledge confession. There was insufficient evidence to convict and the conviction was quashed.

(3) Emotion as corroboration

Sometimes the expression of an emotion can corroborate. There are only two main examples of such an occurrence; (1) distress and (2) surprise.

Distress

Distress can corroborate lack of consent in sexual assault and rape cases. Lack of consent in such cases is an essential ingredient of the offence (one of the *facta probanda*) and so must be proven by corroborated evidence. In such cases, the principal evidence will almost always come from the complainer who will provide an account of the offence. Where the complainer exhibits distress shortly after the offence and this is witnessed by another, the account of the distress offered to the court by that other witness can be used to corroborate lack of consent. This is because the evidence of distress is independent of the evidence from the complainer. However, there are limits to this idea. A bench of five judges in *Smith v Lees* (1997) confirmed that distress can corroborate lack of consent in a sexual assault case, but that it cannot corroborate what happened. It was held that where someone is distressed, it can be implied that what has happened to that person was distressing, therefore confirming or supporting the allegation by the complainer that he did not consent. However, there must be corroboration of the *facta probanda* in the libel, and this cannot come simply from the distress of the victim where it was not contained in the evidence of the principal source (usually the complainer).

A further limitation arises from the timing of the exhibition of distress. Normally, the evidence of distress arises from distress exhibited very shortly after the alleged offence. However, in *McCrann v HMA* (2003), the evidence was that the complainer became distressed around 14 hours after the alleged attack in circumstances where she had, shortly after the incident, returned home but failed to mention the matter to her adult son. In addition, she had gone to work the next day and seemed "happy and relaxed" until, at 1pm, she broke down following a telephone call. It was held that the distress in this case came too late and could not corroborate the lack of consent 14 hours earlier. The High Court pointed out that there was no fixed interval after which distress was incapable of corroborating consent, the position would vary from case to case.

Surprise

The exhibition of surprise operated as corroboration in the case of *Fulton v HMA* (2000). There, the accused was convicted of possession of an illegal firearm. The police had raided the flat where the accused and his landlord lived. During the raid, the police found a shotgun in a cupboard. When it was discovered, the landlord was present. According to evidence given later from one of the police officers, the landlord had looked "genuinely shocked". There were only two people living in the flat and who therefore would have had access to the cupboard—the accused and the landlord. It was held that the surprise exhibited by the witness indicated that he knew nothing about the presence of the shotgun. The landlord gave evidence that he had seen the accused with the shotgun on a prior occasion outside the flat. This was the principal evidence of possession. The surprise at the later finding of the shotgun in the cupboard confirmed and supported this. There was a strong (and persuasive) dissenting judgement in this case from Lord Coulsfield. In fact, the conviction in this case was quashed by a bench of five judges following a referral to the High Court by the Scottish Criminal Cases Review Commission (*Fulton v HMA* (2005)). However, the High Court did not criticise the view that surprise could corroborate. They reached the view that it should not in this case, as a result of arguments not canvassed during the original appeal.

Other emotion or reactions

There would seem to be nothing in principle to prevent the courts in the future from holding that some other emotion or reaction could act as corroboration.

(4) Corroboration of identification evidence

As stated above, the Crown must establish by corroborated evidence that the accused committed the crime. We have already dealt with some particular problems arising out of sufficiency and identification. On the question of corroboration, it seems that where there is one emphatic identification, little else is required to corroborate it. This is demonstrated in the case of *Ralston v HMA* (1987). This case involved an allegation of assault and attempted robbery of a security van guard. There were three witnesses who gave identification evidence. The first was the guard assaulted by the accused. His identification was positive and emphatic. The second guard failed to identify the accused in court, but had picked him out of an identity parade on the basis that he resembled the perpetrator. The third guard pointed the accused out in court but did so by saying "I could not say for definite but it is possibly him...". It was held that there was sufficient corroborated evidence of identification in this case, with particular reference made to the positive emphatic identification.

(5) The Howden exception

Normally, in a case where there is more than one charge on a complaint or indictment, the Crown must corroborate the identification of the accused in relation to each separate charge. However, there is an exception to this rule and this was provided in the case of *Howden v HMA* (1994). The accused was convicted of committing two robberies, one of a building society and one of a bank. There was no question over the sufficiency of the identification evidence in relation to the building society robbery. However, the three witnesses who witnessed the bank robbery were unable to positively identify the accused. It was held, however, that there were some similarities between the two offences, and these were such that the jury were entitled to conclude (as they did) that the person who committed the building society robbery also committed the bank robbery. Eight points of similarity were identified. These related mainly to clothing, conduct and things said by the perpetrator of each robbery.

Therefore, where the court is satisfied that (1) the accused committed the crime libelled in one charge and (2) due to similarities between the circumstances of the offences, the same person must have committed both offences, the court can find there to be sufficient evidence of identification in relation to both charges, even if the identification evidence in relation to the second charge would normally be, on its own, insufficient.

This exception to the corroboration rule has been confirmed more recently in the case of *Gillan v HMA* (2002). In that case, the exception did not apply. Although there were similarities between the circumstances of the offences, these were not similarities that were relevant to the identification of the accused, so *Howden* was not in point. However, the High Court in this case gave some examples of features that could, if similar in relation to both charges, allow the *Howden* rule to be applied, namely evidence of the perpetrator of both crimes being of a similar height and build, of wearing similar clothes, or of speaking similar words.

(6) The Moorov doctrine

This is a very important exception to the corroboration rule. While finding its origins in the writings of Hume, the modern statement of this concept is to be found in the case of *Moorov v HMA* (1930). This device is similar in nature to the *Howden* rule (above) in that it allows evidence from one charge on the complaint or indictment to be used to corroborate another charge in the same complaint or indictment. This time, however, the similarities relied upon are not those relating to the identification of the perpetrator (as is the case in the *Howden* rule) but instead are those that relate to the offences themselves.

Lord Justice-General Clyde in *Moorov* sets out the classic definition of the doctrine:

> "[in order for the doctrine to apply]...the connection between the separate acts (indicated by their external relation in time, character or circumstance) must be such as to exhibit them as subordinates in some particular and ascertained unity of intent, project, campaign or adventure, which lies beyond or behind- but is related to- the separate acts."

Accordingly, two basic conditions must be met before this doctrine can apply:

1. The separate acts must be connected by time, character or circumstance (or a combination of two or indeed all three of these); and
2. There must be some underlying campaign or adventure connecting the acts, as evidenced by this connection(s).

Where two charges are connected by the *Moorov* doctrine, the doctrine allows the evidence in one of the charges to corroborate the evidence in the other and vice-versa. In almost all *Moorov* cases, there is only one source (the complainer) to implicate the accused and nothing else. The operation of *Moorov* provides the corroboration of that account. The corroboration lies in the connection plus the project or campaign.

There are a number of subsidiary points that should be made about the application of this doctrine which will demonstrate its scope.

Identification on each charge

The accused must be positively identified by at least one witness on each relevant charge for the doctrine to apply.

Different offences

The offences to be connected are not required to be of the same name; the importance lies in the similar nature of the offences. For example, in *Carpenter v Hamilton* (1994), the two charges were breach of the peace and indecent exposure. However, the time, place and circumstances of the offences were connected, so the *Moorov* doctrine was applied. Similarly, in *P v HMA* (1991), the doctrine operated to allow mutual corroboration between offences of rape and sodomy, the connection lying in the conduct of penetrative sexual abuse of children.

Passage of time

The passage of time between each pair of offences that are sought to be connected by *Moorov* is important, and is often fatal to the application of the doctrine. This is not because there is a *requirement* that the offences be connected closely in time (note the reference in *Moorov* to time, character *or* circumstance). However, for there to be an underlying project or campaign, a close connection in time is usually required. The courts have been unwilling to lay down a particular time limit, each case will depend upon its own facts. Some brief examples should provide a flavour:

- *Coffey v Houston* (1992), two years not fatal.
- *Turner v Scott* (1996), almost three years "borderline".
- *Bargon v HMA* (1997), three years, seven months too long.
- *McCrae v HMA* (2005), three years, three months not fatal.

As a general rule of thumb, it appears that a gap of up to two years will usually be tolerated. A gap of three years or more will usually be too long. A gap of between two and three years will be a "grey area" for the operation of the doctrine.

However, the courts have emphasised time and again that there is no fixed rule on the period. This was confirmed by the High Court more recently in the case of *Dodds v HMA (2002)*.

In that case, two other points were made about time lag:

1. The time between the last incident and the trial is irrelevant—it is the period between the offences that matters—in that case the numerous offences were alleged to have occurred between 1969 and 1978 and the trial occurred in 2002.

2. Lord Justice-Clerk Gill commented on an *obiter* basis (by relying on the judgement in *Moorov* of Lord Sands) that where the two crimes are of "particularly unusual similarity", the *Moorov* doctrine might apply even where the time lag between them was lengthy.

Greater corroborates lesser but not vice-versa

Where the *Moorov* doctrine is relied upon to provide corroboration between two or more charges, and where the charges involve different crimes, the court will allow the more serious charge to corroborate the less serious but the less serious may well not operate to provide corroboration for the more serious charge. This happened in *HMA v Brown* (1969), where the charges were of two types—lewd practices and incest. It was held that the incest charges could corroborate the charges of lewd practices, but not the other way around, since incest was a much more serious charge than lewd practices. See also *Hutchison v HMA* (1988), where it was held that a breach of the peace charge could not corroborate a charge of indecent assault where the latter charge involved physical contact and force.

Failed Moorov cases

The *Moorov* argument is not, by any means, universally successful and the High Court has shown a willingness to keep the doctrine strictly within its limits.

For example, in *Farrell v Normand* (1993) the High Court ruled that *Moorov* did not apply where one of the offences involved an element of indecency and where the other did not, although both were breach of the peace charges where the offences had been committed over a short period in premises on the same street in Glasgow.

In *HMA v Cox* (1962), the doctrine was not applied as between a charge of sodomy and one of incest, since the charges were different. Two crimes of incest did not corroborate one another either due to the passage of three years between them, despite the fact that these were crimes alleged to have been committed by the accused against his step-children.

In *Dodds v HMA* (2002), the High Court held that both time lags and dissimilarities operated to exclude the applicability of the doctrine as between a number of pairings involving a total of seven charges of rape.

A good example of a borderline case is that of *Hay v Wither* (1988), where the two charges were of breach of the peace. One involved the accused approaching a 14-year-old male youth from behind in public toilets in a park and embracing him. The second involved the accused approaching a 16-year-old male youth in a neighbouring park around three and a half months later and asking him for sex. In each case, the offender drove off in a van. It was held that the *Moorov* doctrine applied in this case.

(7) Statutory exceptions to the rule requiring corroboration

Sometimes Parliament will provide that corroboration is not required in certain circumstances. For example, some statutory provisions allow certain routine evidence to be uncorroborated where the accused will not challenge it:

- s.281 of the 1995 Act, pathologist and forensic scientist evidence.
- s.282 of the 1995 Act, evidence as to controlled drugs.
- ss.283–284 of the 1995 Act, video and fingerprint evidence.
- s.281A of the 1995 Act (which came into force, April 1, 2005), the person picked out by the witness in an identification parade

will be presumed to be the same person as the accused at trial where they have same name.

On occasions where the persuasive burden is on the accused to establish a defence, corroboration of his statutory defence is required (*Templeton v Lyons* (1942)—truancy case and reasonable excuse defence). However, where the statutory burden on the accused is evidential only, uncorroborated evidence will do (*Farrell v Moir* (1974); *King v Lees* (1993)).

(8) Silence or dishonesty of accused

While these can be taken into account to assess *credibility* they cannot usually provide *corroboration*. In *Fisher v Guild* (1991) the court found that the accused had lied when he claimed that he did not know who the driver of the vehicle was at the relevant time. The High Court held that there was sufficient corroboration in this case, but that this did not, and could not, come from the lies told by the accused. Lord Justice-General Hope said this of the evidence:

> "No doubt [his evidence on this point] was a lie, but this is not to say that it was an admission that the [accused] was in fact the driver of the car. It was a worthless piece of evidence which the sheriff should have left out of account."

It has been held, however, that where the accused named someone else as being the driver of a car at the relevant time, and where this was proven to be false by other evidence, this lie was sufficient to corroborate (*Winter v Heywood* (1995)). Although this case has been followed recently, the High Court has made it clear that it is not happy with the *Winter* decision and has hinted that it would be prepared to convene a bench of five judges to reconsider it (*Brown v HMA* (2003)), and so it seems that *Winter* might be reversed in the future.

On the question of silence, it is clear that this can offer no corroborative value, since it has no evidential value at all. Lord Justice-General Cooper put it this way in *Robertson v Maxwell* (1951):

> "...no legitimate inference in favour of a prosecutor can be drawn from the fact that a person, when charged with crime, either says nothing or says that he has nothing to say. He is entitled to reserve his defence and is usually wise if he does so."

However, the right to silence is not absolute. The main exceptions are:

- Recent possession of stolen goods; silence could be a "criminative circumstance" (*Fox v Patterson* (1948)—see earlier).
- *Brown v Stott* (2001)—ECHR case—obliged to incriminate oneself under s.172 of the Road Traffic Act 1988.

(9) Circumstantial evidence and corroboration

Corroboration can be provided by the use of such evidence. *Walker and Walker* devotes an entire chapter to circumstantial evidence (Chapter 6), which is defined there as:

> "...not in itself directly probative of an issue, and in order for it to be of evidential value the court must be able to draw an inference from it which supports that issue." (See also Hume, Commentaries, ii, p.384, approved by Lord President Rodger in *Fox v HMA* (1998)).

Walker and Walker then goes onto deal with certain examples of circumstantial evidence, such as possession of incriminating articles, forensic evidence, print evidence, distress of the victim and reactions of the accused. Therefore, circumstantial evidence is not direct evidence (an example of which would be evidence from an eye witness) but is evidence that is indirectly incriminating.

The role of circumstantial evidence can be even more prominent than acting as a source of corroboration. A case can be based purely on such evidence. Where an inference of guilt can be drawn from all of the circumstances, and as long as such evidence comes from at least two sources, there is no need to corroborate each of the *facta probanda* individually—the circumstantial evidence may be enough. In this way, this represents an exception to the usual corroboration rule. In such cases, the adminicles of circumstantial evidence build up a picture which, when taken together, allow an inference of guilt to be drawn, even although there is no direct evidence of the accused's involvement in the crime. Good examples of such cases include *Little v HMA* (1983) and *Norval v HMA* (1978).

(10) Corroboration and DNA or Fingerprint evidence

It seems that where the DNA or fingerprint of the accused is found in a place or on an object to which the accused would not normally innocently have access to, and where the place or object is connected with the crime, there will be regarded as being a sufficiency in the absence of an innocent explanation by the accused. This would appear to be an exception to the corroboration rule. However, it is not really dealt with as such by the courts. This situation is not recent and it arose in cases such as *HMA v Rolley* (1945) (accused's palm print on furniture at the scene of a break in); *Langan v HMA* (1989) (accused's fingerprint in the blood of the deceased on a tap inside the victim's home where she was murdered). More recently, an accused person was convicted as a result of his DNA being found to be on a mask worn by the robber and left at the scene, and where the mask had the DNA of others on it and it had been made out of the sleeve of a woollen jersey (*Maguire v HMA* (2003)).

There are two possible explanations for this idea. The first is that such a case is one based purely on circumstantial evidence (see above on this). The second is that it is one of those special cases where there are facts peculiarly within the knowledge of the accused, and so there arises a presumption of guilt, in similar vein to the doctrine of recent possession of stolen goods, dealt with earlier. Neither explanation is explicitly approved in the cases, although the courts do seem to be hinting at the latter in some places.

ADMISSIBILITY

In this part, we will deal with the following:

1. Admissibility generally.
2. Admissibility of hearsay evidence.
3. Admissibility of evidence illegally or improperly obtained.

ADMISSIBILITY GENERALLY

Where a party in a criminal case wishes to argue that an anticipated piece of evidence is inadmissible, an objection will have to be made at the appropriate time. The judge or sheriff then (or later) decides if it is to be allowed and his decision can be appealed—in borderline cases, a wrong decision to include such evidence can be fatal to a conviction.

There are four possible reasons to argue that evidence in a criminal case should be declared inadmissible:

4. It is irrelevant.
5. It contravenes the best evidence rule.
6. It contravencs the rule against hearsay evidence.
7. It has been obtained improperly.

We will now deal with each of these in turn.

Relevance

Evidence must be relevant in order to be admissible. This may seem obvious and usually it is. The general test has been expressed as follows:

> "...the ultimate test is whether the material in question has a reasonably direct bearing on the subject under investigation" (Lord Osborne in *Strathmore Group Ltd v Credit Lyonnais* (1994)).

Although this is a civil case, the test is equally applicable in criminal cases.

There are three main issues that arise on the subject of relevancy in criminal cases; collateral evidence, character evidence and sexual history evidence. Each will now be dealt with in turn.

Collateral evidence

Sometimes such evidence is known as "similar fact evidence". It comprises evidence of something outwith the circumstances of the charge(s) being considered by the court. The general rule is that such evidence is inadmissible. The idea behind this rule is that evidence of a similar incident or of similar behaviour is irrelevant to the question of whether, on the occasion in question, the accused behaved in a particular way. This rule is an example of the general rule that irrelevant evidence is inadmissible. The rationale of excluding such evidence was explained by Lord Justice Clerk Ross in *Brady v HMA* (1986) as follows:

> "The general rule is that it is not admissible to lead evidence on collateral matters in a criminal trial. Various justifications have been put forward for this rule. The existence of a collateral fact does not render more probable the existence of the fact in issue; at best a collateral matter can only have an indirect bearing on the matter in issue; a jury may become confused by having to consider collateral matters and may have their attention diverted from the true matter in issue. Whatever the justification for it the general rule is clear"

Exceptions to the rule

Some of the exceptions to this general rule have already been dealt with. Two of these have already been considered; the *Moorov* and *Howden* rules. In a way, these rules allow evidence to "bleed" from one charge to another to provide a sufficiency.

Even where the evidence is coming from outwith the charges faced by the accused, there are some exceptions to the general rule. Under the 1995 Act, ss.274–275, sexual history evidence suggesting consensual sexual contact between the accused and the complainer, or even between the complainer and a third party, might be admitted (see below).

In certain circumstances, where there is a very close connection between an earlier act by the accused and the charge in question, the court might allow evidence of the earlier behaviour to be admitted. In *Dumoulin v HMA* (1974), evidence of fraudulent transactions in Germany was admitted on the basis that these transactions were "an integral part of the preparation for the commission of the crimes libelled...". Such instances will, however, be rare and only where the evidence of the earlier offence (which is not being prosecuted) is absolutely necessary for background purposes will it be admitted. See also *HMA v Joseph* (1929), a decision of Lord Murray in the High Court. However, where the two incidents are closely related, evidence of the one not being prosecuted may be admissible.

Where the evidence of the other incident is being led in order to try and establish that, having behaved in a particular way in the past, the accused is more likely to have behaved in the same way on the occasion in question, the general rule will apply and the evidence will be excluded. In

Nelson v HMA (1994), the Crown sought to lead evidence from a police officer that when the accused was being arrested, he ran into a toilet and swallowed a small cellophane-wrapped object. He was being prosecuted for being concerned in the supply of controlled drugs under the Misuse of Drugs Act 1971. Objection was taken to this evidence on the basis that it would involve leading evidence of an offence not being pursued—that of obstructing the police by trying to conceal possession of controlled drugs—a specific offence under s.23 of the 1971 Act. The evidence was, it was argued, collateral. The High Court disagreed. The evidence of attempted concealment was directly relevant to the charge in question and was therefore admissible. The Crown was not seeking to establish that the offence of concealment under s.23 had been committed.

Character evidence

Character of the complainer

Usually, evidence of the general character of the complainer is irrelevant and so inadmissible. The same rationale is employed as that for collateral evidence—just because the complainer has behaved in a particular way in the past does not mean that he has done so on the occasion in question. Once again, the provisions on sexual history evidence in the 1995 Act (dealt with below) represent an exception to this rule.

A further limited exception concerns violent conduct. The scope of this exception was explained by Lord Justice Clerk Ross in *Brady v HMA* (1986):

> "...in cases of murder or assault it has been decided that an accused may prove that the injured party was of a quarrelsome nature or violent disposition but that he may not prove specific acts of violence committed previously by the injured party."

Of course, it must be established that the violent character of the complainer is in some way relevant to the case. Most commonly, the argument being pursued by the accused is that he was acting in self-defence. In order to succeed in that defence he must establish that he acted proportionately in response to the attack by the complainer. A general violent disposition toward the accused might be relevant to the establishment of this defence. However, in such a situation, evidence of a violent disposition toward third parties will be regarded as not falling within the exception and will be excluded as truly collateral—see *Brady v HMA* (1986).

There is one other wrinkle in this area. Although evidence of prior specific acts of violence will usually be inadmissible, where the Crown *set out in the wording of the complaint or indictment itself*, their intention to establish that the accused was previously violent toward the complainer, this might allow the accused to lead evidence of previous specific attacks by the complainer on him. This was the situation in *HMA v Kay* (1970), however, such cases will be rare.

Character of the accused

As before, the general rule is that evidence of the general character of the accused is inadmissible, and again, there are some exceptions, this time principally statutory exceptions.

The general rule is to be found in the 1995 Act, s.266(4). The accused may not be asked questions tending to show his bad character or that he has previous criminal convictions, unless in certain circumstances:

1. where proof of a previous conviction is necessary to proof of the offence being considered by the court (s.266(4)(a));
2. where the accused has already given evidence against a co-accused (s.266(4)(c));
3. where either the good character of the accused or the bad character of a Crown witness, or both, is made an issue by the accused (s.266(4)(b)).

Examples of the first situation include charges of driving while disqualified (proof that an offence leading to disqualification was committed is implicit) and prison-breaking where the accused was serving a sentence at the time (where the accused can be asked about the conviction that led to the sentence).

The second situation is self-explanatory.

The third situation, if it arises, will allow exposure of both the previous criminal record of the accused (if any) as well as the general character of the accused. The third situation will arise where the accused himself gives evidence, or if any witness called by him gives evidence (or both) of the good character of the accused, or even where Crown witnesses are asked to comment on the accused's good character. In addition, where the nature of the defence is such that it involves imputations on the character of the prosecutor or any Crown witnesses, or the complainer (*i.e.* where the complainer is not a Crown witness) the usual protection afforded to the accused will be lost. However, it should be noted that something more than accusing a Crown witness of lying will be required in order to constitute an attack on the character of that witness, hence exposing the accused's character or convictions. What is required is an allegation of some more sinister conduct on the part of the witness. The line between the two is not always clear (*Sinclair v MacDonald* (1996)).

Normally previous convictions cannot be divulged, and this protection is specifically provided for—see s.101 and s.166 of the 1995 Act. While the protection here is closely guarded, the accidental exposure by the Crown of details of the prior convictions of the accused will not always be fatal to a conviction in the case in question—see *McCuaig v HMA* (1982).

Finally, it should be noted that even where the accused does not give evidence at the trial, his character and criminal record can be attacked by the Crown in largely similar circumstances in terms of s.270, and the conditions set out there.

Sexual history evidence

There is one area of the criminal law where the role of the concept of relevance has always been highly controversial—that of sexual history and sexual character evidence. The present law on this form of evidence is contained in ss.274–275 of the 1995 Act. The original provisions of the 1995 Act were amended in 2002 (Sexual Offences (Procedure and Evidence) (Scotland) Act 2002, s.7 and s.8). The 2002 amendments essentially involved the insertion of two new provisions in place of the old ss.274–275. These new provisions came into force on November 1, 2002. The result is a change to the rules, particularly the procedural rules, that govern the raising of such questions.

The basic position is that there is a general prohibition in sexual offence cases on questions that are designed to establish that the complainer:

1. is not of good character (sexual or otherwise);
2. has at any time engaged in sexual behaviour not forming part of the charge;
3. is likely to have consented to the acts forming part of the charge or is not a credible or reliable witness because he has at any time engaged in non-sexual behaviour, unless that behaviour has occurred shortly before, at the same time or shortly after the acts that form the subject matter of the charge;
4. is likely to have consented to the acts forming part of the charge or is not a credible or reliable witness due to the witness suffering from any condition or predisposition.

It will be seen that this prohibition is limited in its effect. A number of exceptions are built into s.274, in other words, cases where the general prohibition does not apply. Section 275 goes on to provide a set of general exceptions to the prohibition in s.274. It should be noted that these exceptions operate in addition to the s.274 built-in exceptions. The s.275 exceptions essentially allow the accused to make an application to the court to allow questioning that would otherwise be prohibited by s.274. The court must be satisfied, in order to grant the application, of three matters:

1. the evidence or questioning will relate to a specific occurrence(s) of sexual or other behaviour or to specific facts showing the complainers character or condition or predisposition to which the complainer is subject; and
2. that the occurrence(s) is relevant to the offence charged; and

3. that if the evidence is admitted, its probative value is likely to outweigh any risk of prejudice to the proper administration of justice.

The "proper administration of justice" includes the "appropriate protection of a complainer's dignity and privacy".

It is difficult to see whether or not the above should lead to any change in the approach to be taken by the courts from that taken under the less detailed and widely worded former ss.274–275 in dealing with such evidence. At the time of writing there are only a handful of reported cases on the new ss.274–275. However, the cases decided under the provisions pre-2002 will continue to be relevant.

In *Cumming v HMA* (2002), an application had been made to lead evidence relating to an incident where the complainer had, at a family event, sat on the accused's knee (along with certain other evidence). He was facing 11 charges of lewd, indecent and libidinous practices and behaviour or indecent assault. Lord Carloway refused the application in connection with this evidence, on the basis that an isolated incident such as this was "totally remote" from the issues in the case and that its admission "appears irrelevant and is probably an affront to the complainer's dignity". The High Court disagreed and held that the evidence would have significant probative value and would not involve material prejudice to the proper administration of justice.

In *Kinnin v HMA* (2002), the Crown, when the case came before the High Court, did not support the decision of the sheriff, who had refused the defence application to lead evidence under s.275. The evidence was that within the month prior to the alleged rape, the complainer had on one or two occasions suggested to the appellant's son that she wished to have a sexual relationship with him (the son). The High Court agreed with the Crown that this evidence could be led under s.275, since all of the conditions were satisfied. The background of comments were made to the son of the accused, not to the accused himself, but the basis of the application was that the evidence would be indicative that the complainer was someone who was "willing to engage in adulterous relations".

Some of the pre-2002 cases will be relevant here. One example is the case of *Bremner v HMA* (1992). There, the accused in a rape trial sought leave to question the complainer on whether the relationship between the accused and the complainer had involved regular sexual intercourse. The relationship had lasted for six months and had come to an end some eight months before date of the alleged rape. The trial judge disallowed the questioning, given the period of time between the ending of the relationship and the date of the alleged rape. The High Court upheld that decision, but appeared rather reluctant to, and did so only on the basis of the fact that this was a matter for the discretion of the trial judge. It is unclear whether a similar decision would be made under the new provisions, but it is likely that it would not.

In *Thomson v HMA* (2001), the evidence sought to be led included evidence suggesting that the complainer had made previous allegations of rape against others, including medical staff at a hospital. The trial judge refused the evidence, stating that these were broad allegations, not of a specific type, and made during a period when the complainer was under stress. The High Court again indicated (as it had in *Bremner*) that although a different judge might have allowed the evidence, it could not be said that the refusal to do so was a course that no reasonable judge would take. It is likely that under the new provisions a similar decision would follow from similar facts.

Procedural provisions
The 2002 amendments do make some radical changes to the procedure to be followed under s.275. One major change is that the application to lead sexual history evidence must now be made in writing and in advance of the trial at a preliminary diet, first diet or intermediate diet. Under the old provisions, the application could be made orally, and had to be made during the course of the trial. In addition, the legislation is specific on the material to be covered in the application (s.275(3)) and on the ground to be covered by the court's written decision (s.275(7)). This process carries the advantages of greater transparency and less likelihood of delay at trial caused by perhaps lengthy legal debate on an application. It also forces the applicant and the court to focus in a precise written way on the issues to be covered.

ECHR and sexual history evidence
As with hearsay evidence under s.259 (dealt with below) the courts have made it clear that the issue of admission of evidence under s.275 may raise the question of a possible breach of the accused's Article 6 rights. However, while such a question can, in some cases, be addressed before the start of the trial (see the English case of *R v A (No.2)* (2002) on the equivalent English provisions), the usual course would be for any such issue to be resolved during the trial (*e.g.* see *Moir v HMA* (2004) in the Privy Council).

The 2002 provisions were challenged under the Convention in *MM v HMA* (2004). There, the High Court held that the provisions were compatible with Article 6, given that they represented a balance between an absolute prohibition and judicial flexibility.

The Best Evidence Rule
This rule requires that primary evidence (the actual article or document) be produced rather than secondary evidence (*e.g.* a replica, substitute or oral description of the article, or copy or oral description of the document) when two conditions are met:

1. where it is reasonably practicable for the primary evidence to be produced; and

2.   where the failure to produce the primary evidence would lead to material prejudice on the part of the other party.

Condition (1) was held not to have been fulfilled in the case *Anderson v Laverock* (1976). There, the accused was convicted of an illegal salmon fishing charge after being found in possession of salmon. He was taken to the police station with the fish which were examined there by the police. The fish were destroyed by the police the following day. It was argued that the absence in court of the fish was fatal to the conviction since the non-production breached the best evidence rule. However, the High Court held that the sheriff was entitled to find (as he did) that, since the fish were perishable, it was not "practicable and convenient" to retain them. The appeal was, however, allowed on another ground.

Condition (2) was unsatisfied in the case of *McKellar v Normand* (1992). There, the accused was convicted of the reset of a bed and blanket found in her home. The bed and blanket were not produced in court and neither were labels in their place. Lord Justice General Hope made these general comments:

"It is good practice for items which are the subject of charges of this kind to be produced if it is convenient to do so or, failing production, for labels relating to the items to be produced in their place. But the question must always be, if an objection is taken as to the admissibility of the evidence, whether in the absence of the items or labels relating to them some injustice is likely to result to the accused."

In this case, it was held that there was no suggestion that any prejudice was being caused by the absence of the items or by the absence of labels representing them. The argument failed, as did the appeal.

It has been made clear that condition (2) above will not be satisfied merely on the basis that the party claiming to have been prejudiced indicates that the presence of the best evidence *might* have allowed some cross examination to take place—the party will have to establish precisely what the prejudice would be (*Kelly v Allan* (1994)).

The best evidence rule applies to documents as well as to real evidence and is again subject to the two conditions explained above. For example in *Nocher v Smith* (1978), the non-production of an original search warrant was not fatal to a conviction on the basis that there was evidence led that indicated that the police officers executing the warrant had acted properly. There was no suggestion, again, that there had been any prejudice caused.

(2) ADMISSIBILITY OF HEARSAY EVIDENCE

The general rule

Walker and Walker defines hearsay evidence as "...evidence of what another person has said (orally, in writing or by other physical expression)" (at para.8.1.1).

For example, where A witnesses an assault and tells B about it, if B is then called as a witness to speak to the conversation, B will be giving hearsay evidence (even if A also gives evidence in the same trial).

In civil cases such evidence is admissible but in criminal cases only *primary hearsay* is admissible—*secondary hearsay* is inadmissible. This general rule was approved by a bench of nine judges in the case *McCutcheon v HMA* (2002).

Rationale behind the general rule

The rationale of the rule is that hearsay evidence is not the best evidence available of what was expressed. It is sometimes viewed as an example of the best evidence rule. This means that the other party does not have the opportunity to cross-examine the person(s) who made the statement or had the conversation.

Also, the witness's demeanour is lost—the court cannot judge whether or not the witness is credible if he is not giving evidence himself—see *Teper v R* (1952) (English case) per Lord Normand on this generally.

Distinction between primary and secondary hearsay

The distinction between primary and secondary hearsay is rooted in the *purpose* of leading the evidence. If the purpose is to prove the *truth* of the statement content, this is secondary hearsay and inadmissible in criminal cases. If the purpose is simply to establish the *content alone,* (and not whether the content is true or false) this is primary hearsay and is admissible in criminal cases as evidence of the statement. Some cases will illustrate this distinction.

In *McLaren v McLeod* (1913), the accused was charged with the offence of brothel-keeping. The prosecution sought to lead evidence from certain police officers of conversations they had overheard. These conversations were between female occupants of the house and reference was made during these conversations to the accused introducing "short time" to the house. The use of this phrase was indicative of the status of the house as a brothel. This evidence from the police officers was objected to as hearsay. The objection was repelled and the accused convicted. In upholding that conviction, the High Court held that the evidence led was primary hearsay and was therefore admissible, as the court was concerned not with the truth or otherwise of the statement, but with the fact that it was made.

McLeod v Lowe (1991) concerned a statement made to police officers who had gone to a hotel to investigate a possible Misuse of Drugs Act offence. Staff at the hotel directed the officers to the bar and pointed out the accused, who was approached and taken to the police station for the purposes of conducting a personal search. The Crown attempted to lead evidence from the police officers as to why the hotel staff had pointed out the accused. This was objected to on the basis that it was hearsay evidence. At first instance, the objection was sustained and the evidence excluded. However, the High Court held that the sheriff had wrongly excluded the evidence, which was primary, not secondary hearsay—the evidence was to the effect that the police received certain information from the hotel staff about the accused and there was no attempt in leading that evidence to seek to prove the truth of it. The appeal was argued principally on another ground and was continued for further evidence to be heard.

Finally, in *Ratten v R* (1971)—an Australian case decided ultimately by the Judicial Committee of the Privy Council—the disputed evidence consisted of a recording of a call made by the murder victim to the emergency services at around the time of the incident. The caller was distressed and asked to be connected to the police. There was evidence to suggest that, at the time of the call, there was no one else in the house other than the accused. The court took the view that the evidence of what the victim said during the call was admissible as primary hearsay evidence—it was not, as the defence claimed, led in order to assert something beyond the words used *i.e.* that the accused attacked the victim.

Some examples of statements held to be or accepted as being secondary hearsay evidence can be found in the cases below, such as *Gibson, Murray* and *O'Hara*, all of these being cases on the *res gestae* exception.

Exceptions to the rule against secondary hearsay evidence

Primary hearsay statements are always admissible in criminal cases. Secondary hearsay statements, as a general rule, are not. However, there are exceptions to that general rule, in other words cases in which even secondary hearsay evidence is admissible.

These exceptions are as follows:

1. *res gestae* statements;
2. statements by the accused;
3. statutory exceptions.

We will deal with each in turn.

Res gestae statements

The *res gestae* exception allows secondary hearsay to be admitted where:

"...a statement is made contemporaneously with an action or event which is or forms part of the fact or facts in issue by a person present at that action or event. The *res gestae* may be defined as the whole circumstances immediately and directly connected with an occurrence which is part of the facts in issue" (*Wilkinson*, p.39).

This concept was commented upon further as follows by Lord Normand in the English case of *Teper v R* (1952):

"[the words must be] if not absolutely contemporaneous with the action or event, at least so closely associated with it, in time place and circumstances, that they are part of the thing being done, and so an item or part of real evidence and not merely a reported statement."

The rationale for the *res gestae* exception is the high value of a spontaneous statement often delivered under pressure, as the examples that follow show.

In *R v Gibson* (1887), a witness gave evidence that just after being struck by a stone, a woman going past the accused's door said, in pointing to his door: "the person who threw the stone went in there". It was held that the words were uttered not as a direct result of the woman seeing the assault, but as a direct result of the accused absconding from the scene. So, the statement (an example of secondary hearsay) was not part of the *res gestae* so the general rule applied and the evidence was inadmissible. In other words, the statement, to qualify as admissible as being part of the *res gestae*, must be inspired directly by the event itself, not some other cause.

In *Murray* (1866), the mother of the accused could testify as to what the accused uttered—described as a "cry of distress"—as it was the first statement she made when returning home. The statement maker could not give evidence as she was deemed an incompetent witness (dealt with elsewhere). This statement was regarded as part of the *res gestae*. This case also demonstrates that hearsay evidence can consist of a sound or exclamation uttered by someone, as opposed to words (see the reference in the *Walker and Walker* definition, above, to "other physical expression").

O'Hara v Central S.M.T. Co (1941) was a case decided at a time when hearsay evidence was inadmissible in civil cases, so it is relevant here. This case concerned an accident involving a bus. The bus had swerved, it was claimed, in order to avoid striking a pedestrian who ran in front of it. As a result of the accident, one of the passengers on the bus sued for damages for personal injury after being thrown from the bus. The driver had attended to the injured person and returned to the bus. A man was there when he got back and he admitted to having ran across in front of the bus. He could not be traced as a witness in the civil action, so the court had to consider whether the driver's account of the "confession" by this man was admissible as part of the *res gestae*. A period of around ten minutes had elapsed between the time of the accident and the statement being made by the man back at the bus. It was held that although there was a time gap involved, the incident was so clearly bound up with the events constituting the accident that they were part of the *res gestae*. In commenting generally on the scope of this exception, Lord President Normand stated:

> "The principle on which evidence of *res gestae*, including hearsay evidence, is admitted is that words and events may be so clearly interrelated that the truth can only be discovered when the words accompanying the events are disclosed. But it is not essential that the words should be absolutely contemporaneous with the events... what is essential is that there should be close association, and that the words sought to be proved by hearsay should be at least *de recenti* and not after an interval which would allow time for reflection and for concocting a story."

Where the crime is one that is committed over a period of time, such as being concerned in the supply of drugs, a statement made by someone else which indicates involvement in selling drugs on the part of the accused, can be regarded as part of the *res gestae*—see the comments of Lord Philip in *Hamill v HMA* (1999).

Res gestae statements should be distinguished from *de recenti* statements, the latter of which are admissible, but only as primary hearsay. *De recenti* statements are those uttered soon after the crime but are not regarded as part of the crime itself. Evidence of the terms of such statements is admissible but not for the truth of them.

In *Cinci v HMA* (2004), the High Court doubted the classic statement on *res gestae* made by Lord Normand in *O'Hara* (above). There, the appellant was found guilty of rape. He appealed, partly on the basis that the trial judge had misdirected the jury on the effect of a statement allegedly made by the complainer to a third party. When the third party found the complainer and accused together, naked, in a shower, the complainer was alleged to have said; "he raped me". The court held, without hesitation, that this statement was not part of the *res gestae*, contrary to the decision of the trial judge, since it was uttered after any sexual intercourse was over. In reaching this view, Lord Justice Clerk Gill and Lord Kirkwood doubted the—technically *obiter*—comments of Lord President Normand in the earlier civil case of *O'Hara v Central SMT* (1941) (see above), where he suggested that the words in question did not have to be "absolutely contemporaneous" with the event and suggested that the words could be "at least *de recenti*". Both judges were keen to send out a signal that the borderline between a *res gestae* statement and a *de recenti* one should be reconsidered, with a view to perhaps widening the *res gestae* exception, to bring the law more in line with English evidence law. The law in this area might, then, be altered in a future suitable case. However, at present, Lord President Normand's comments stand.

The question of whether a statement is part of the *res gestae* or a *de recenti* statement will depend upon the circumstances of the individual case. The main use of *de recenti* statements is in sexual assault cases, where they are often used to evidence lack of consent (see, *e.g. Morton v HMA* (1938)).

Statements by the accused

Evidence from another witness on what the accused has said on an earlier occasion will constitute hearsay evidence. There are three types of statement that an accused person may make: a confession, a self serving statement and a mixed statement.

Confessions are generally regarded as admissible at the instance of the prosecution, (unless obtained unfairly—discussed later) as a confession is a statement made against interest, and so is usually reliable.

A self-serving statement is sometimes referred to as an exculpatory statement; either way, such a statement is one that suggests that the accused is innocent. The position on self-serving and mixed statements will now be dealt with.

Exculpatory statements relied upon by the accused

The courts have formulated a specific rule to cover this situation. The rule was more recently affirmed by a bench of nine judges in the case of *McCutcheon v HMA* (2002) who all concurred in an opinion delivered by Lord Justice General Cullen, who expressed the position in this way at paragraph 16 of the judgement:

> "The main rules which apply are as follows: (i) It is a general rule that hearsay, that is evidence of what another person has said, is not admissible as evidence of the truth of what was said. (ii) Thus evidence of what an accused has been heard to say is, in general, not admissible in his exculpation, and accordingly the defence are not entitled to rely on it for this purpose. Such evidence can be relied on by the defence only for the purpose of proving that the statement was made, or of showing his attitude or reaction at the time when it was made, as part of the general picture which the jury have to consider...."

Therefore, hearsay evidence of the accused led by the defence can only be led for these limited purposes. This is to prevent the accused using an earlier statement as evidence of the truth of what is said, and in doing so, seek to avoid giving oral evidence, thereby avoiding cross-examination of his account. If the accused wishes the court to accept the *truth* of his account, he will have to give oral evidence on it. This rule is, however, a slight extension of the general rule (above) which either rules out or allows hearsay evidence on the basis of whether it is primary or secondary hearsay. Instead, in the case of the accused, there are certain legitimate purposes of leading a statement other than simply showing that the statement was made; the attitude or reaction of the accused can be one of those purposes.

Mixed statements

A more difficult area is the admissibility of a "mixed statement". Essentially, a mixed statement is one that contains some material that is exculpatory of the accused (suggests that the accused is innocent), as well as materially incriminating the accused.

The question of whether a statement is mixed or not is not as straightforward to answer as it might first appear. For example, in *Lennox and Boyle v HMA* (2002), the charge against both appellants was being concerned in the supply of drugs contrary to the Misuse of Drugs Act 1971, s.4(3)(b). The Crown relied on certain statements provided by both appellants admitting possession of the drug, as well as other evidence which might be regarded as evidence of a supply operation. In their statements, both appellants denied selling the drugs and insisted they were for personal use only. The sheriff indicated in part of his direction to the jury that the statements were exculpatory. The High Court held that this was a misdirection since the statements were clearly mixed and the convictions were quashed.

The case of *McIntosh v HMA* (2003) demonstrates that even High Court judges can disagree on the fundamental issue of whether a statement is mixed or not. In this case, the appellant had been found guilty of murder by stabbing. At the time of the offence he was 15 years old. The appellant was, at the time, detained in a residential school. A few days after the murder, he had a conversation with a care worker in which he stated that he had been at the scene of the murder when it happened with a friend. He told his care worker that his friend had attacked the deceased, stabbed her repeatedly and ran off, leaving him at the scene with the victim. At the trial, the appellant sought to incriminate his friend. The trial judge took the view that the statement was entirely self-serving and the appellant's "admission" that he had been at the scene at the time of the murder was made only to set up his exculpatory explanation. Mere attendance at the scene could not be, in itself, incriminatory and the rest of the statement was clearly exculpatory.

The appeal court, however, did not agree. The Lord Justice Clerk in referring to the need for a wider consideration of the other evidence available stated:

> "In my opinion, the question does not depend on the appellant's purpose in making the statement, nor on the Crown's purpose in leading evidence on it…The test is whether the statement, considered objectively, was in any way incriminatory in its effect. In my opinion, the statement, although intended to be exculpatory, was nonetheless incriminatory in three material respects. First, it put the appellant at the scene of the murder at the time it was being committed. Second, it did so in the context of several witnesses who

said that they saw only one youth in the vicinity of the locus at the material time. Third, it represented a significant change in the appellant's previously consistent account that he had been alone [in the relevant wooded area]."

This view was shared by Lords Kirkwood and MacLean who issued separate judgements. In the end, however, the conviction was upheld. The court refused to agree that there had been a miscarriage of justice, since, despite the misdirection, the other evidence against the accused was "compelling". See also *Jones v HMA* (2003).

The rule on mixed statements

Assuming that the statement is properly classified as a mixed one, the applicable rule was again confirmed by the bench of nine decision in *McCutcheon v HMA* (2002). Lord Justice General Cullen, delivering the unanimous opinion of the court, put it this way at paras 16–17:

> "The main rules which apply are as follows:...[rules (i) and (ii) are reproduced above] (iii) There is, however, an exception where the Crown have led evidence of a statement, part of which is capable of incriminating the accused. The defence are entitled to elicit and rely upon any part of that statement as qualifying, explaining or excusing the admission against interest."

In other words, where a statement is a mixed statement led by the Crown, the accused is entitled to rely upon it as evidence in support of his defence and not just for the limited purposes of, *e.g.* credibility, or to show that the statement was made, but also in order to establish the truth of the statement or part of it.

Accordingly, it can be important for the defence to establish that a statement is a genuinely mixed one. This can lead to the rather strange situation in which the defence is arguing that a statement contains incriminating and exculpatory parts while the Crown argues that the statement is purely exculpatory.

Statutory exceptions

The main statutory exceptions to the hearsay rule are to be found in ss.259 and 260 of the Criminal Procedure (Scotland) Act 1995. It should be noted that, with limited exceptions, these provisions are inapplicable to hearsay statements by the accused (s.261 of the 1995 Act).

Section 259 statements

This section allows the admission of hearsay evidence in certain common circumstances.

Four conditions must be fulfilled before the statement of a person can be admissable under this section. These conditions are set out in s.259(1)(a)–(d):

(a) the person who made the statement will not give evidence in the proceedings for one of five specified reasons (see below);

(b) evidence of the subject-matter of the statement would be admissible if the maker of the statement were to give direct oral evidence of it. There must, in other words, be no other exclusionary rule which affects the statement. For example, if a statement is regarded as protected by a legally recognised privilege (privilege is dealt with elsewhere), it will not be admissible under s.259. Also, the question of whether the evidence would have been relevant to the charge might arise—see *HMA v Beggs (No.3)* (2001), where the question was whether the evidence if allowed would have been collateral to the main issues. It was held that it would not have been so this condition was satisfied;

(c) the maker of the statement would have been a competent witness at the time the statement was made—see *Patterson v HMA* (2000), where the issue was whether the now deceased witness, having admitted to an alcohol problem and having indicated that she was under the influence of alcohol when having made the statement, was a competent witness. It was held that she was competent, as the restricted grounds of incompetency of a witness did not apply;

(d) there is sufficient evidence that a particular statement was made, and is either contained in a document or is one of which the person giving evidence has direct personal knowledge. The requirement of "direct personal knowledge" prevents the admission of so-called "multiple hearsay" under this section (which is permitted by the Civil Evidence (Scotland) Act 1988 for civil cases). Multiple hearsay evidence is evidence that has been passed through one person or more before it reaches the ears of the witness giving evidence.

The five specified reasons, one of which must exist before condition (1) above is satisfied, are to be found in s.259(2):

1. the witness is dead or is bodily or mentally unfit to give competent evidence;

2. the witness is outwith the UK and cannot reasonably practicably attend or tender his evidence in any other competent way;

3. the witness cannot be found after reasonable steps have been taken to find him—see, *e.g. Aslam v HMA* (2000), where the sheriff's decision (not disturbed by the High Court) deals with the question of reasonable steps to find a witness and *Hill v HMA* (2005), where the High Court found that reasonable steps had not been taken;

4. the witness refuses, contrary to a court ruling on the issue, to give evidence since he may incriminate himself;
5. the witness refuses to take the oath or refuses to give evidence on the content of the statement, having been directed to do so by the judge—in the case of a child witness, the condition is only satisfied if the child is directed to answer, otherwise this part of s.259 is not activated (*MacDonald v HMA* (1999)).

As long as one of these five reasons applies, causing the original statement maker to fail to give evidence on the statement, hearsay evidence of the statement may be led as long as conditions (b)–(d) above are also satisfied. Of course, the terms of s.259 need only be invoked where the statement would otherwise be inadmissible as secondary hearsay. If the statement would constitute primary hearsay evidence, it is admissible anyway under the general rule (above).

Finally, it should be noted that where any of the five situations described above are *engineered*, the evidence not admissible (s.259 (3)).

Section 259 and notice
In most cases, a party intending to lead evidence in terms of the provisions of s.259 must give notice. There are notice and counter notice provisions, along with certain exceptions (s.259(5)–(7)).

Section 259 and discretion
It is clear that where the conditions of s.259 have been met, the court has no discretion to refuse the admission of the hearsay evidence. Once the relevant conditions have been met, the statement is automatically admissible (*Nulty v HMA* (2003); *Daly v HMA* (2003)).

However, it has been held that since s.259 represents a substantial innovation in the law of evidence and that its terms must be interpreted and applied strictly. So in a situation where hearsay evidence would be admissible but the court has not followed s.259 strictly, the evidence may not be allowed (this situation would normally occur on appeal)—see *MacDonald v HMA* (1999).

Section 259 and human rights
A number of cases have been decided by the High Court on the question of whether the use of s.259 by the Crown—in order to introduce the hearsay statement of a witness—breaches the accused's right to a fair trial, protected by Article 6 of the ECHR. Particular focus in these cases has rested on the right enshrined in Article 6(3)(d), which provides that everyone charged with a criminal offence has the right to examine or have examined, witnesses against him. Given the lack of discretion where the conditions of the section are met (see above), a challenge under Article 6 is one well worth considering in any s.259 case.

It is clear that s.259 does not, in itself, breach Article 6 (*McKenna v HMA* (2000), *HMA v Nulty* (2000) and *HMA v Bain* (2002)). This applies even where the hearsay evidence represents the sole corroborating source (*Campbell and Hill v HMA* (2004)). The basis appears to be that the Scottish legal system incorporates protections for the accused that, when taken together with s.259, (as opposed to looking at that section in isolation) offer sufficient protection of the right to a fair trial. These protections include the right to cross-examine the witness making the statement, the requirement of corroboration and the protection incorporated in s.259(4), the latter allowing the statement, once admitted, to be challenged in the normal fashion. However, in any individual case, depending upon the circumstances, an attempt to invoke s.259 *might* breach Article 6. Again, these three cases make this clear. In fact the trial judge must, throughout the trial, consider whether the impact of the evidence is infringing the accused's right to a fair trial under Article 6, and if he so finds, he may uphold a submission of no case to answer on that basis or desert the trial. (*Nulty,* supported by *Campbell and Hill*). This might even mean taking a decision on this point in advance of the trial, although this would be exceptional (*Nulty*; *HMA v M* (2003)).

Section 260 statement
Where a witness gives evidence, a prior statement made by the witness is admissible under s.260 of the 1995 Act as evidence of any matter covered in the statement, as long as certain conditions are met. These conditions are:

1. The statement being referred to must be contained in a document (s.260(2)(a));
2. The witness must indicate during the course of his evidence that the statement was made by him (s.260(2)(b));
3. He must also indicate, again during the course of his evidence, that he adopts the statement as his evidence (s.260(2)(b));
4. He must have been a competent witness at the time the statement was made (s.260(2)(c));
5. The statement must be one that would not be admissible otherwise than under this section (s.260 (3)).

If all of these conditions are met, the prior statement may be put to the witness under s.260.

The common law position was similar, under the case of *Jamieson v HMA (No.2)* (1995), which can still be relied upon. One difference between the common law and statutory positions is that the *Jamieson* case applies only where the witness is unable to recollect events, and where an earlier statement is used to fill the gap. The statutory provisions allow the use of the prior statement in wider circumstances. There is no need to establish lack of recollection; a statement could be put to a witness who claims to recall events, but where the earlier statement (usually given to police) is different to that being relayed in oral evidence (although here s.263(4) could be used—see below). Another difference is that under the statutory provision, the prior statement must be in writing, while in terms of *Jamieson*, there is no such restriction.

Another important provision is s.263(4). This provision allows a party to put an earlier statement to a witness, where the witness said something in the statement which differed from that said in the witness box. This time there is no requirement that the statement is made in writing (unlike under s.260). Also, this provision can be used to challenge the evidence of any witness, including the accused, unlike s.259 and s.260 (see s.261).

Meaning of statement for the purposes of s.259 and s.260—precognition
The word "statement" is defined in s.262(1) for the purposes of s.259 and s.260 as:

> "(a) any representation, however made or expressed, of fact or opinion; and
> (b) any part of a statement,
> but does not include a statement in a precognition other than a precognition on oath."

This definition is important, since it excludes the use of either section in connection with a prior precognition. A precognition is an account of events that is not a *verbatim* (word for word) account using the words of the witness, it is an account taken from the witness but put into words by someone else. Parliament has excluded such documents from the ambit of both sections so that a precognition taken from the witness cannot be used as a prior statement. The objection to the admissibility of a precognition was articulated by Lord Justice-Clerk Thomson in the case of *Kerr v HMA* (1958):

> "..what is of importance...and one reason why reference to precognition is frowned on is simply that in a precognition you cannot be sure that you are getting what the potential witness has to say in a pure and undefiled form. It is filtered through the mind of another whose job it is to put what he thinks the witness means into a form suitable for use in judicial proceedings. This process tends to colour the result. Precognoscers as a whole appear to be gifted with a measure of optimism which no amount of disillusionment appears to damp."

Usually, it will be obvious when a document is a precognition, but sometimes it will not be. For example, in the civil case of *Highland Venison v Allwild* (1992), a solicitor had taken details of an incident from a witness at a meeting in London. She then prepared a draft precognition and sent it to the witness for signature. The witness (who died before the hearing) retyped the document, and in doing so he incorporated certain amendments to it, signed it and then sent it back to the solicitor. Lord

Cullen in the Outer House held that the document started off as a precognition but then ended up as a statement due to being re-typed and signed by the witness. Although this is a civil case, it is applicable in criminal cases.

Where a police officer is making enquiries generally of a witness and details are taken, the result will probably be regarded as a statement, but where the officer is taking statements on the instructions of the prosecutor, these are more likely to be regarded as precognitions (see the cases of *HMA v Irving* (1978) and *Kerr v HMA* (1958) for examples of both situations).

There are two ways around this exclusion where a party wishes to introduce evidence deriving from a precognition. One way is to lead evidence of the conversation between the precognition taker (perhaps a solicitor) and the witness by leading the precognoscer in oral evidence. The exclusion in s.262(1) only covers putting the precognition itself to the witness—an oral account of the conversation is not excluded—as long as it does not fall foul of any other admissibility rule, such as the hearsay rule. In fact, the precognoscer could even refer to the precognition as an *aide memoire* before giving evidence, as long as certain conditions are met (see the case of *Deb v Normand* (1997) on the use of an *aide memoire*, regarding the notebook of a police officer). Although there appear to be no direct criminal authorities on this avoidance route, the courts in interpreting a very similar civil evidence exclusion (Civil Evidence (Scotland) Act 1988, s.9) have held that such a manoeuvre is perfectly competent (see Lord Clyde in *Cavanagh v BP Chemicals* (1995), Lord Morton of Shuna in *Anderson v Jas B Fraser & Co Ltd* (1992), affirmed by Lord Hardie in *Ellison v Inspirations East Ltd* (2003)). Although these are civil cases, they will apply in criminal cases, since the general objection to the admissibility of precognitions (outlined in *Kerr*, above) is the same in either situation.

The second way around this exclusion is to simply rely on s.263(4) of the 1995 Act, if that subsection applies. The definition of "statement" as applied to s.259 and s.260 (as contained in s.262(1), which excludes a precognition) does not apply to a statement under s.263(4). Hence, the precognition itself can be put to a witness under s.263(4). This loophole (if it can be described as such) does not appear to have been argued in *HMA v Al-Megrahi (No. 2)* (2000), where the High Court and the parties dealt with the case on the basis that a statement in a precognition is inadmissible under s.263(4).

Common law application—deceased witness
In cases where the statutory provisions (s.259 or s.260 of the 1995 Act) are not relied upon (perhaps because the relevant conditions do not apply), the statement of a deceased witness can be admitted, even if it is in the form of a precognition, at common law. However, the common law rule provides that where the precognition is taken from a witness who has

some interest in the events spoken to in the precognition or where litigation is, at the time of the taking of the precognition, in contemplation, the evidence will be inadmissible. For examples, see *William Thyne (Plastics) Ltd v Stenhouse Reed Shaw (Scotland) Ltd* (1979) (an internal memorandum written after intimation of a claim was declared inadmissible), and *Pirie v Geddes* (1973) (a conversation by telephone between a police officer and the complainer, the latter of whom died before the trial, was refused admission on the basis of self-interest by the statement maker). For an example of a case where there was held to be no self interest, see *Moffat v Hunter* (1974) (two statements made by an eye-witness to an insurance company at a time when no claim was intimated and where the witness was unaware of the reason for the involvement of the insurance company). Although these cases are civil cases, the same principle applies in criminal cases (*Walker and Walker*, para.8.7.1).

(3) ADMISSIBILITY OF UNFAIRLY OR IMPROPERLY OBTAINED EVIDENCE

This is a major category of inadmissibility in criminal cases. The general rule is that if evidence is not obtained properly and fairly it could be inadmissible even if otherwise perfectly competent and relevant.

In general, there are two categories of evidence for the purposes of this section:

- real or documentary evidence; and
- incriminating statements by the accused (also referred to as confessions).

We will deal with each in turn. However, we must first consider briefly the underlying approach of the courts in all such cases.

THE GENERAL APPROACH—A BALANCING ACT

In both situations, the guiding principle is fairness. This involves the balancing of the liberty of the individual which should not be invaded illegally or irregularly by the authorities, against the interests of the state in securing evidence in order to prosecute crimes so that relevant evidence should not be excluded on the basis of a technicality. The classic case on this balancing act is *Lawrie v Muir* (1950), which has been cited in numerous cases since. Essentially, this principle involves the proposition that evidence will not be excluded automatically just because there is some irregularity in the method by which it was collected—an irregularity can be and will be overlooked if the balancing act referred to above requires it.

For example, in *Hoekstra v HMA (No.5)* (2002), the Crown conceded that the placing of a tracking device on a ship during a drug surveillance operation was illegal. However, they argued that this illegality should be excused in the circumstances of the case. The High Court agreed, and repelled the objection to the admissibility of the drugs seized during the operation. It was made clear that the fact of the deliberate placing of the device did weigh heavily against the admission of the evidence gathered once the ship was intercepted. On the other hand, the court pointed to the limited role the tracking device had played in the case—no evidence had been derived directly as a result of the placing of the device—as well as the fact that there was already a substantial body of other evidence concerning the likely use of the ship for drug carrying purposes.

It is clear then, that the balancing act will lead to different results in different cases, depending upon the circumstances. However, these cases can be categorised and some general guidance can be gleaned by examining some examples.

(1) REAL AND DOCUMENTARY EVIDENCE

These cases involve the gathering of evidence by a search. The search is normally conducted by police officers, but it should be noted that other officials have, in certain circumstances, the power to search, *e.g.* officers of HM Customs and Excise, Inland Revenue officials and immigration officials.

Has a search been conducted at all?

Sometimes the question that arises is whether a search has been carried out at all. If there has been no search, the issue of the legality of the evidence recovery process will not arise. For example, in one case, a nightclub doorman requested that a patron empty his pockets. On doing so, the patron produced some tablets which the doorman took possession of. This was held not to have been a search—see *Mackintosh v Stott* (1999). In *HMA v Megrahi (No.3)* (2000), it was held that there had been a search where the police had, while interviewing a witness, "a look round the premises" and as a result took possession of a diary that belonged to one of the accused, although the evidence was, in the end, declared admissible. In *Graham v Orr* (1995), the Crown argued that the constable was merely checking inside the car of the accused to see if there was anything to explain the accused's suspicious behaviour. The High Court held that as soon as he opened the door of the car, the constable was searching it, and the drugs found were inadmissible in evidence, since the search had been conducted illegally.

A question of authority

Where there has been a search, the search is usually conducted by the police (or other official) to find evidence in either a property owned or occupied by a suspect, or on the person of the suspect. The general rule is that the official carrying out the search must usually have *authority* to search. There are two possible sources of authority:

1. Statutory provision; or
2. Warrant.

(1) Statutory authority

There are many examples but two main ones will suffice for our purposes—drugs and weapons.

Under the Misuse of Drugs Act 1971, s.23(2) and (3), a police constable has the power to search a person, vehicle, vessel, or premises (the latter only with a warrant) if he has *reasonable grounds to suspect* that the person is in possession of controlled drugs or holds controlled drugs on the premises.

In the case of weapons, under the Criminal Law (Consolidation) (Scotland) Act 1995, s.47 it is an offence to have an offensive weapon in a public place. A constable has the power of search under s.48 if he has *reasonable grounds for suspecting* that someone is carrying one and that and that a s.47 offence has been or is being committed. Similar provisions in ss.49–50 cater for offences of possession of an article with a blade or point.

These two examples have been chosen since most cases on the power of search involve the question of whether or not the official had *reasonable grounds to suspect* possession of an illegal item or substance. It is not enough that the official does suspect. If there are no *reasonable grounds* to suspect, then the search is illegal and any evidence relating to the seized item(s) or their seizure will be excluded. This will usually be fatal to the Crown case in any drugs or offensive weapons prosecution, since the existence of the drugs or the weapon must be established, as well as possession of the illegal item in the hands of the accused. If the Crown cannot refer to the relevant production(s) during the case, they will not be in a position to secure a conviction.

Some cases on "reasonable grounds to suspect"

There are numerous examples of these, so a select few should provide a flavour of the approach by the courts. It should be noted that the High Court has made it clear that there are no hard and fast rules and that the question is always one of fact and degree in any particular case.

Where the information giving rise to the suspicion in the mind of the constable is out of date, reasonable grounds to suspect may not be found to have existed. This was what occurred in *Ireland v Russell* (1995). In that case, the police information was some two months old and could therefore not justify a search. The court made it clear, however, that there was no definite time limit on information of this kind—much would depend on the circumstances of the case.

A different result ensued in *Weir v Jessop (No.1)* (1991). There, the search was under s.23 of the 1971 Act. The police had searched a suspect and found him to be in possession of controlled drugs. They had received a call from a member of the public who informed the police that someone (unidentified) was involved in the misuse of drugs on the fourth landing of a particular block of flats. On attending there around five minutes after the call, they found the suspect alone on the landing referred to by the caller. The police asked him if he had been involved in using drugs and he replied "no", but went on to volunteer that he had been involved with drugs in the past. He was then searched and the drugs were found. The High Court held that the constables did, in all of the circumstances, have reasonable cause to suspect that the accused was in possession of drugs. The search was therefore proper and the appeal against conviction was refused.

In *Houston v Carnegie* (2000), the question of reasonable grounds to suspect arose under s.14(1) of the 1995 Act, which contains a general power to detain a person on suspicion that he has committed an offence punishable by imprisonment. The accused had been standing in the company of a suspected drug dealer at around 10pm in a public street. The High Court, in quashing the conviction of possession of drugs with intent to supply, held that this did not constitute reasonable grounds to suspect, and the detention was therefore unlawful.

This case is also interesting from a more general perspective. The constable in question had not, it was held, applied his mind to the question of whether there were reasonable grounds to suspect. He had merely been ordered by a superior officer to detain the accused. The High Court held that the test is objective, and that the constable does not require to satisfy himself that the test has been met, only the court can later determine that, and the (subjective) view of the constable is irrelevant in answering that question.

While the *Houston* case is not a case concerning a search, but instead the legality of a detention, the phrase "reasonable grounds to suspect" was interpreted, so the case is relevant here.

Where the power of search includes the power to search any vehicle in which the suspect is travelling, it is implied in such a power that the police can also search any passenger in the vehicle, even where the reasonable grounds to suspect only relate to one occupant in the vehicle. This was the decision of the High Court in *Cooper v Buchanan* (1997), another case under s.23 of the Misuse of Drugs Act 1971.

It is clear that behaviour of a generally suspicious character alone may well not be sufficient to give rise to reasonable grounds to suspect. In other words, the constable must, before the search can be legally carried out, have come to suspect the accused of having committed an offence (*Graham v Orr* (1995)).

One final point worth noting is that the requirement of the existence of reasonable grounds to suspect applies only to police officers, not to others, *e.g.* nightclub doormen—see *Mackintosh v Stott* (1999).

(2) Warrant

The second source of a power to search for real or documentary evidence comes generally from a warrant. A warrant is a document, usually signed by a judge, that gives the police the power to search premises. Where the search is of an individual, the reasonable grounds to suspect test will usually apply, and no warrant will be required. Therefore, the vast majority of warrant cases relate to the search of premises.

Personal searches and warrants

It is important to note, however, that a warrant can be obtained to search an individual. This will usually be done where the search required is of an invasive character, such as for the taking of dental impressions (*Hay v HMA* (1968)); of blood samples (*HMA v Milford* (1973)); for an internal search of drugs concealed within the body of the suspect (*Vaughan v Griffiths* (2004)); or the taking of bodily measurements (see the unusual case of *Smith v Cardle* (1994), where the measurements were allowed to be taken from someone who was not even an accused person or suspect in relation to the relevant charge). The authorities have made it clear that in such cases the balance is between the public interest in the prosecution of crimes on one the hand, and the invasion of privacy of the suspect on the other (*Hay v HMA* (1968)—full bench).

Although not yet tested in this context, the right to respect for private life under Article 8 of the ECHR may well be argued in the future in such cases, since it has been made clear by the European Court of Human Rights that this right covers the "physical and moral integrity of the person" (*X and Y v The Netherlands* (1986)).

In addition, there are certain statutory provisions that authorise the taking of fingerprints and samples of certain material from an accused person, principally someone who has been detained under s.14 of the 1995 Act or has been convicted of an offence in certain circumstances (see ss.18–20 of the 1995 Act).

Searches of premises and warrants

A warrant is usually required in order to search the premises of a suspect, or indeed of another person. In the vast majority of cases involving the search of premises, there will be a statutory provision authorising the search but requiring a warrant in order for the search to be regular. One of the most common examples is a search for drugs under the Misuse of Drugs Act 1971. Under s.23(3), a search warrant is required before premises can be searched.

Where a warrant is required by statute (or where it is required by common law in the case of a personal search—see above), there are generally three types of situation that arise:

1. An argument that the warrant itself is defective;
2. An argument that the warrant is valid, but that its terms have been exceeded;

3. An argument that the warrant is valid, but that the premises searched are not the premises specified in the warrant.

Situation 1— the defective warrant

Here, it is argued by the accused that there is some defect in the warrant which is fatal to its validity and therefore the material found in the search has been illegally seized and is inadmissible in evidence. The courts will entertain and uphold such an argument, but only in connection with serious irregularities in the warrant itself; minor ones will be overlooked.

For example, in *HMA v Cumming* (1983), a warrant was granted for the search of premises under the Misuse of Drugs Act 1971, s.23. There were various formal defects in the warrant, and the Crown and defence presented a joint motion to the sheriff seeking a determination at a preliminary hearing as to the validity of the warrant. The sheriff held that the warrant was defective and in doing so held that some of the defects could be excused, while others could not. The accused had been described in one part of the warrant as "James Cumming" and in another as "John Cumming" (the latter being correct). Since no confusion existed as to the identity of the accused, this was held to be a defect that could be excused. The same applied to the failure by the justice of the peace (who granted the warrant), to fill in the date on the pre-printed warrant form—the date had been specified elsewhere in the warrant. However, the failure to insert the name of the officer to whom the warrant was granted was described as a "much more serious matter". The failure to specify an officer was in direct breach of the stringent terms of s.23(3) which require that the warrant has to authorise any constable acting for the police area that the premises are situated in, to conduct the search. Finally, there was no specific description of the premises to be searched; on the warrant, the printed words "said premises at" were followed by a blank. The sheriff could not accept that the mention of the premises earlier in the form was sufficient, and this was held to be a fatal defect also.

In *Bulloch v HMA* (1980), search warrants obtained under the Finance Act 1972 in connection with an investigation into VAT evasion allegations were declared invalid since they were undated. This is against a background of a statutory execution time limit for the warrant of 14 days, and without a date, there was no way of telling the date from which this period was to run. Therefore, anyone approached in order to execute the warrant would have had no way of knowing if the warrant was still valid. It was argued by the Crown that evidence could be led to establish when the sheriff had granted the warrant, but Lord Ross (the trial judge) rejected this approach.

In *HMA v Bell* (1985), the High Court had to consider the validity of a warrant which was not signed at the foot and was not dated. Once again, this was a warrant issued under s.23 of the 1971 Act. It was held that the warrant was invalid. The name of the justice had been completed by her in a space provided in the body of the warrant, but the failure to subscribe was held to be fatal. The court went on to hold that the lack of a date would not have been fatal in this case had the warrant been subscribed.

Finally, it appears that an argument suggesting that the defects in a warrant are excusable on the ground that the warrant was sought urgently, will not be regarded as persuasive (*HMA v Cumming* (1983)).

Situation 2—warrant exceeded; extent of search
Where the warrant is valid and specifies the power of search, that power should not be exceeded, otherwise the material found will be inadmissible. Most cases here involve accidental finds.

It is clear that where a search is being carried out under a warrant and where certain items or documentation are being sought, where the searchers "stumble" by accident upon other incriminating material, the latter material will be admissible. However, where the find is not accidental, the terms of the warrant have been exceeded, and this may lead to the evidence uncovered being declared inadmissible. For example, in *HMA v Turnbull* (1951), a tax fraud case, officers had attended at the office of the accused, an accountant, with a search warrant authorising a search for documents relating to a butcher client of the accountant. A large amount of documentation was removed, including documentation relating to the affairs of other clients of the accused, as well as those relating to the butcher client. Following on from this, the accountant was charged with a number of offences of fraud and attempted fraud. Lord Guthrie, the High Court trial judge, relied on four considerations in holding that the warrant had been exceeded. First of all, there was no urgency involved in the execution of the warrant (see below on urgency). Secondly, the actions of the police in retaining material irrelevant to the investigation was deliberate, not accidental—they had retained the documentation for six months—in any event the incriminating character of the documents could only be discovered upon a close examination, the material was not plainly incriminating. Thirdly, the officers had seized *private* material and then examined it to see if any criminal charges should be brought; if there was any information implicating the accused in any further crimes, a wider search warrant could have been sought. Fourthly, he relied on the principle of fairness in coming to the conclusion that the deliberate seizing of private papers in order to then investigate a possible crime for which the police had no evidence before the search, would breach the general rule of fairness to the accused. The objection to the admissibility of evidence was sustained and the accused was acquitted.

It has been made clear by the High Court that the constables conducting a search must be aware of the extent of the warrant when the search takes place. In *Leckie v Miln* (1981), the constables conducting the search had not seen the search warrant, which was part of a petition containing two charges of theft. They knew that the accused was alleged to have committed acts of theft, but they were not aware of any of the details. They were allowed entry to the premises by a co-habitee of the accused and found certain incriminating items. The High Court ruled that the search was clearly random. The officers did not know, in advance of the search, what was alleged to have been stolen, and the search was conducted with a view to finding items that would support evidence of a theft of any kind, not just those libelled in the petition.

Conversely, in *Drummond v HMA* (1993), the officers searching the premises were aware of the nature of the charges and were searching the accused's house under a warrant for stolen furniture. Items of clothing, similar to those stolen in another incident, were found during the search in a wardrobe on the premises. These items were taken and were to be referred to in connection with the proceedings on the clothing theft charge. The High Court declared the evidence admissible since one of the officers gave evidence that he was looking in the wardrobe for items of furniture and simply came across the items of clothing. The search was therefore conducted within the terms of the warrant.

It seems that where a house is being searched under a warrant in connection with a supply of drugs case, and where the police suspect that a person in the house is engaged in the supply of drugs, someone who arrives at the house who can offer no innocent explanation for his presence there, may be searched on the basis of reasonable grounds for suspicion of a drugs offence—see *Guthrie v Hamilton* (1988).

A further example, this time of a warrant based on a charge of a statutory offence, is the case of *Burke v Wilson* (1988). Here, the search warrant covered a search in the shop of the accused for any video tapes which bore no classification under s.10 of the Video Recordings Act 1984. During the search, certain videos were found which were of a pornographic nature. This led to a charge of possessing obscene video tapes with a view to selling them under s.51(2) of the Civic Government (Scotland) Act 1982. It was held that, since the find was accidental, the evidence was admissible, despite the fact that the search was for a different purpose, in connection with a different statutory charge.

There is one major limitation to the idea that items accidentally found during a search under warrant can be used in evidence on another charge not covered by the warrant. The evidence "stumbled across" must be of a "plainly incriminating character" (*Drummond v HMA* (1993); *HMA v Turnbull* (1951)), or at least of a "very suspicious character" (Lord Guthrie in *HMA v Hepper* (1958)). In other words, the police may not simply seize items that they stumble across that are of an innocuous character in the hope of tying them up later to a different crime from that covered by the warrant.

Situation 3—wrong premises

Clearly, a property search warrant will specify the location of the premises to be searched. This is crucial, given that, if the property actually searched is different to that described in the warrant, the fruits of the search are likely to be declared inadmissible. Clearly, cases in which the completely wrong premises are included in the warrant by mistake will be rare. The more common cases are those where there is some doubt over the proper *extent* of the warrant, as it operated within a particular premises.

For example, in *McAvoy v Jessop* (1988), the search warrant authorised the search of a premises occupied by a named individual, not the accused. The premises consisted of a flat where individual rooms were occupied by different persons—the accused only occupied one room at that address. During the search, the room occupied by the accused, as well as the one occupied by the individual named on the warrant, were searched. In the accused's room, a stolen video recorder was discovered, which led to a charge of reset (a charge the accused was later convicted on). The High Court held that the irregularity in this search could not be excused. The officers could not reasonably have taken the view that the warrant covered a room at the same address occupied by someone other than the person named in the warrant and the conviction was quashed.

A different situation arose in *Guthrie v Hamilton* (1988). Here, the warrant authorised the search of a house and anyone found in it, in connection with a misuse of drugs investigation. While the officers were conducting the search, the accused came to the front door of the house and knocked. The door was answered by one of the officers and the accused made to enter. He was then searched. It was held that the warrant covered this search and the drugs found on the accused's person were admissible. The High Court therefore refused the appeal and upheld the conviction. They did so on the basis that the search warrant covered not only the house but also the garden ground, the path leading to the front door and the front doorstep. Anyone found in these areas could, therefore, be searched under the warrant.

The role of urgency

In various cases, the courts have made it clear that one of the circumstances that will be taken into account in considering whether a search should have been carried out is whether or not there was any urgency in the collection of the material. Sometimes this question arises in cases that do not involve a search warrant (see, *e.g. HMA v Hepper* (1958)). However, in most cases in which urgency plays a role, incriminating or suspicious material unconnected to the investigation has been accidentally found ("stumbled upon") during a search for other material under a warrant. The question then, is whether the police should leave the premises in order to obtain a second warrant that covers the newly found material before seizing it. The courts have made it clear that where this scenario arises, and where a second warrant is not sought, the irregularity in the search (where a warrant covering the new material would normally be required) may be excused on the grounds of urgency. The urgency arises from the danger that the occupier of the premises may take the opportunity, while the second warrant is being sought, to move or destroy the incriminating or suspicious material. An urgency argument was not persuasive in *HMA v Turnbull* (1951), a case dealt with above, while in *Hepper*, also above, urgency did exist. The High Court in *Burke v Wilson* (1988), (above) held that the danger of the pornographic video tapes disappearing if a new search warrant was obtained played a part in the decision that the evidence was admissible.

Human rights in search cases
The right to privacy under Article 8 of the ECHR has given rise to some case law in connection with searches. We have dealt with this right in the context of personal searches already.

In *Hoekstra v HMA (No.5)* (2002), the High Court indicated that, in line with Convention case law, the exclusion of illegally obtained evidence is not necessarily required under Article 8. In *Birse v HMA* (2000), the accused argued that Article 8 had been breached due to circumstances arising from the procedure followed when the warrant was sought from a justice of the peace under s.23(3) of the Misuse of Drugs Act 1971. That challenge failed. See also the similar case of *Ormiston v HMA* (2000) (where a similar result to *Birse* followed), in which *Birse* was applied and in which reference was made, in addition, to Article 6.

(2) CONFESSION EVIDENCE

Many cases have been decided on the basis of confessions rendered in arguably unreliable circumstances. Many decisions in infamous miscarriage of justice cases have been on the basis of confessions being declared inadmissible due to their unreliability, leading to the verdict being rendered unsafe. It should be made clear that the word "confession" is used in this book to refer to *any incriminating statement made by the accused* and not just what is traditionally thought of to be a confession, namely a full account of the crime.

The value of a confession
A confession is a very strong piece of evidence, so the circumstances of its utterance are closely protected by the law. The reason for the high value placed on a confession is that it is a statement against the maker's own interests. Under normal circumstances, a person does not usually confess to a crime that he has not committed (see the exceptional case of *Boyle v HMA* (1976), where the Crown conceded that the confession had been false). This has already been commented on in the context of sufficiency.

Admissibility of a confession—the general rule
The courts have made it clear that the test of the admissibility of a confession is a simple one; has it been extracted fairly?

Lord Justice-General Emslie put it in this way in *Lord Advocate's Reference (No.1 of 1983)* (1984): "The simple and intelligible test which has worked well in practice is whether what has taken place been fair or not?"

In making this comment, the Lord Justice-General was applying the test as formulated by a predecessor, Lord Justice-General Clyde in *Brown v HMA* (1966). This test has been re-affirmed more recently by the High Court in *Codona v HMA* (1996) (including Lord Justice-General Hope).

This test is well established, having received explicit approval not only by the High Court in numerous cases, but by three separate Lord Justice-Generals.

However, it should be noted that the consideration of fairness has been held to involve a balance between fairness to the accused on one hand and fairness to the public on the other hand (see Lord Wheatley in *Miln v Cullen* (1967) and the opinion of the court in *Jamieson v Annan* (1988)). Despite this, the predominance of authority still favours the approach of fairness to the accused (indeed, "fairness to the public" would be an unusual test). More recently, the use of the public interest in considering the admissibility of confessions has been said to be "entirely out of place" (see the opinion of the court delivered by Lord Justice-General Hope in *B v HMA* (1995), in which the reference to "the public interest in the suppression of crime" as part of the charge to the jury was regarded as a fatal misdirection). More recently still, however, the public versus accused interest test has resurfaced, although absent any debate on the propriety if its use (*McIntyre v HMA* (2005)). The author still believes that the test of fairness to the accused alone will prevail, although the law in this area is still unclear.

Although the test benefits from an inherent simplicity, and although it is always the ultimate test in every case in which the admissibility of a confession is challenged, there are certain types of cases in which this test has been applied, and these will now be examined.

Unfair questioning techniques

The test has been most frequently applied in cases where it is claimed that a confession has been unfairly extracted from an accused person by police officers who have secured the confession by employing unfair questioning tactics.

A convenient starting point for an examination of the cases is the "three-stage" sequence adopted by the High Court in *Chalmers v HMA* (1954). In cases where the police questioning methods have come under scrutiny, the *Chalmers* court sets out that there are essentially three stages in the progress of any investigation:

Stage 1: during the investigation, before suspicion falls upon an individual—any question can be asked generally without limit;

Stage 2: after suspicion crystallises on an individual, the rules of fair questioning kick in to protect him;
Stage 3: following charge, any questioning is prohibited.

Stage 2 is by far the most controversial.

The dividing line—stages 1 and 2

It might be difficult to determine precisely when the investigation has progressed from stage 1 to stage 2. It is certainly possible for an investigation to remain at stage 1 even although the accused is one of a defined group of persons under suspicion, as long as he has not become the only one under suspicion—see, *e.g. Bell v HMA* (1945), where the group was the crew of a ship. See also *Miln v Cullen* (1967); and *Pennycuick v Lees* (1992), dealt with below. In *HMA v McPhee* (1966), the witness was described by the police officer who heard the confession as a "mild suspect" and possibly or possibly not a witness; in this case, evidence of the confession was admitted.

Questioning at stage 2

Most case law centres around stage 2. The basic rule at this stage is that any confession obtained must have been provided voluntarily. A major consideration in deciding whether or not a confession has been provided voluntarily, as opposed to having been extracted by unfair means, is whether the questioning process has strayed into the territory of "interrogation" or "cross-examination". If it has, the confession will have been extracted unfairly.

These terms were defined by Lord Justice-General Emslie in *Lord Advocate's Reference (No.1 of 1983)* (1984), where he said:

> "...where in the opinions in the decided cases the word 'interrogation' or the expression 'cross-examination' is used in discussing unfair tactics on the part of the police it is to be understood to refer only to improper forms of questioning tainted with an element of bullying or pressure designed to break the will of the suspect or to force from him a confession against his will."

The category of unfair questioning techniques was expanded in *Codona v HMA* (1996), when the High Court stated that "leading or repetitive questioning" might form the basis of a good argument that the confession had been extracted unfairly. In suggesting this, the court approved the comments (above) of Lord Justice-General Emslie. In a case involving repetitive questioning, it is clear that the repetition would require to be sustained, and that asking a suspect if he is sure of his account would probably not, alone, be enough to affect the admissibility of the confession (*Hartley v HMA* (1979)).

In approaching the question of whether a confession has been extracted by unfair questioning, the courts have taken account of the purpose of the officers in employing a particular method of questioning. Where the purpose of the interview is seen to be to extract a confession, this will strengthen the argument that it has been extracted unfairly. However, where the purpose of the interview is judged as being the carrying out of investigations, the confession is more likely to survive scrutiny (*Chalmers v HMA* (1954); *Tonge v HMA* (1982)). It should be noted, that there does not require to be some "dark" purpose on the part of the interviewer in order that a confession is held to have been tendered in unfair circumstances—the questioner may well be trying to be fair to the suspect—see, *e.g.* the case of *HMA v McSwigan* (1937), where the officers tried to dissuade the suspect from making an incriminating statement. The statement was declared inadmissible due to the circumstances in which it was made (low I.Q. of the suspect who misunderstood the nature of the charge, prompting an explanation that was incriminating). In other words, purpose is only one potential factor.

In *Codona v HMA* (1996), the accused, who was 14 years old, was interviewed by police in a murder investigation. The text of the interview took up 91 pages of transcript. It had lasted for over three hours. During the interview the accused was asked on nineteen occasions whether she had kicked the victim. She denied kicking the victim, until late on in the interview. Also, during the interview, the police told her repeatedly that they did not believe her since her denial was inconsistent with information from elsewhere that suggested that she had kicked the victim. It was held that in all the circumstances, the confession had been extracted unfairly.

On the other hand, in the *Lord Advocate's Reference (No.1 of 1983)* (1984), the court judged that a confession had not been unfairly obtained. The view was taken that the questioning was characterised by "relaxed exchanges" during which the questioning was "polite" and the accused had "quite freely contributed to the flow of the conversation".

In each case, the questions asked and the technique employed will be different, therefore, the use of examples is of limited value. However, it is instructive to read in the case reports in this area the excerpts of interview transcripts.

Caution
Once suspicion has hardened on an individual (stage 2 in the *Codona* analysis, above), but before any questions are asked the accused should be cautioned. If he is not properly cautioned, the answers may be inadmissible. The caution that should be administered is the so called "common law caution" which has two essential elements:

1. The right to remain silent; and
2. Anything said might be used as evidence in court.

There is no prescribed form of words, as long as these two elements are conveyed. In fact, this requirement is so strict that even where a statutory caution was administered properly, this was held not to be a sufficient caution since only the right to silence was required to be mentioned (*Tonge v HMA* (1982), which dealt with the caution provided for under the Criminal Justice (Scotland) Act 1980, s.2 (now repealed); see also *HMA v Von* (1979), in which the failure to mention the right to silence was fatal).

Once again, however, the overall test is one of fairness and so there are some circumstances in which a caution has not been administered but where the confession has been declared admissible. For example, in *Custerton v Westwater* (1987), the complainer alleged to the police that the accused had waved a knife at him. The accused was asked to attend the police station in connection with the allegation and did so voluntarily. After being informed of the allegation, the accused said nothing. He was then asked; "Do you have a knife?", to which the accused then made an incriminating reply. He had not, at this stage, been cautioned. The High Court held that the reply was admissible, despite the absence of a caution. The critical feature for the court in this case was that the reply was not made in response to the allegation, but instead was a reply to an unobjectionable question. Also relevant was the fact that the accused had gone to the police station voluntarily, he had not been summoned there and the police had not visited him.

In *Pennycuick v Lees* (1992), the accused had been questioned on two separate occasions, four months apart, by Department of Social Security officers. He was later charged and convicted of making false statements in order to obtain payment of benefits, a statutory charge under s.55 of the Social Security Act 1986. It was held that on the first occasion, the questions were asked with a view to helping the officers with their enquiries. A caution was not necessary, since suspicion had not yet crystallised on him as someone who may have committed a criminal offence. On the second occasion, a caution was only administered after the accused had been shown—and had admitted to having signed—some claim forms which then were essential productions in the Crown case. Although suspicion had, by this time, crystallised, it was held that since the accused clearly knew what was happening, there was no suggestion of pressure or deception in the questioning and he was on guard, both as a result of the initial interview, and having been told at the outset of the second one what the purpose of the visit was, the failure to administer a caution was not, in all of the circumstances, unfair.

It has been made clear that a caution need not specifically address the potential use of the tape recorded voice of the suspect, taken during his interview, for comparison purposes (*McIntyre v HMA* (2005)).

The physical or mental state of the suspect
Moving away from questioning and cautions, it has been made clear that the physical or mental state of the suspect at the time when the confession occurs is one factor that may be taken into account in deciding if a

confession has been elicited fairly (see Lord Cameron in the single judge decision of *HMA v Gilgannon* (1983)).

Physical state

Where a suspect has just been roused from sleep when the incriminating statement is made, it has been regarded as fair that the accused be woken fully, so that he is aware of what is happening before being asked any questions. The failure on the part of police officers to do this where the accused had been asleep in his car, was fatal to the admissibility of the statement in *McClory v MacInnes* (1992).

Where a suspect was sick, shivering and had to lie down to recover during police interview, this was held as relevant in considering the admissibility of his confession (*HMA v Aitken* (1926)).

If the accused is intoxicated by alcohol, this may form a ground for arguing that a confession has been extracted unfairly. However, evidence of the mere consumption of alcohol prior to the confession is not sufficient. The alcohol must have the effect of rendering the accused incapable of being aware of what he is saying. Such a condition was not suffered by the accused in *Thomson v HMA* (1989), where his confession was held to be admissible. Although there are no reported cases, intoxication by drugs would, no doubt, be treated similarly.

If the suspect is in a state of physical distress, this might render any confession inadmissible (*HMA v Rigg* (1946), where the suspect was described as "excited, partially collapsed, trembling and shuddering").

One can imagine other examples. For instance, if the suspect is physically injured and is in pain, this might be sufficient to be held to have distracted him from his account, or even from the terms of any caution administered. Another example might be a drug addict whose sense of understanding of a caution or of the situation he is in is impaired due to him suffering withdrawal symptoms where some time has passed since his last intake. In such cases, the question will always be whether the confession has been provided in circumstances of fairness to the accused.

Mental state

A metal disorder suffered by the accused at the time of making the statement might be relevant in considering its admissibility. In *HMA v Gilgannon* (1983), a police surgeon had examined the accused five hours before the interview in question and had determined that the suspect was mentally subnormal and was incapable of giving a coherent and complete account of events. Lord Cameron, sitting alone, sustained the objection made by the defence to the admissibility of the confession. He commented that this objection was a good one, no matter how carefully the statement may have been elicited in accordance with "the rules of fair play and proper practice". Having said this, implicit in Lord Cameron's decision is the idea that a mental disability of some sort will not, on its own, be enough. The disability would have to be identified as one that could have (Lord Cameron speaks of "possibly if not probably") a detrimental effect on the ability of the suspect to impart an accurate and complete account of events. Indeed, this was the basis of the decision of the High Court in *Higgins v HMA* (1993), where a suspect suffering from schizophrenia was deemed by the court (on the basis of medical evidence) to be capable of providing a coherent detailed account of events, despite his condition. Medical evidence from the police surgeon who examined the accused shortly after the incriminating statement was made suggested that he was able to understand what was going on. *Gilgannon* was distinguished on its facts.

Something short of a mental disorder might be sufficient to trigger a successful unfairness argument. The mental distress of the suspect could be enough (*HMA v Aitken* (1926)—unable to read over statement due to mental condition; *Chalmers v HMA* (1954)—suspect reduced to tears during questioning).

It has been held that a medically verifiable propensity to suggestibility during an interview might be prayed in aid of an unfairness argument in connection with a confession (*Blagogevic v HMA* (1995), although in that case the challenge failed, this was for procedural reasons, and the court took no adverse view on the line of attack generally). See also *Campbell v HMA* (2004) and the comments on the effect of that case in the section on opinon evidence in part 1, earlier. Suggestibility formed part of an argument in the lower court in *B v HMA* (1995), and again, although the appeal was considered on another ground, the High Court did not comment unfavourably on the admissibility of the evidence of a psychologist on the subject.

Low intelligence can be argued in support of an admissibility argument where this would affect the suspect's understanding of proceedings. For instance, in *LB v HMA* (2003), evidence was presented from a psychiatrist as to the appellant's verbal I.Q. and his ability to understand a caution. A clinical psychologist also gave evidence about research showing that persons of a similar age and ability to the appellant are unable to understand the caution. The appeal did not deal with the admissibility question, but there seems to have been no concern in the appeal court that the evidence was admitted by the trial judge. Where the low intelligence of the suspect affects his understanding of the nature of the charge, leading to a confession prompted by such a lack of understanding, evidence of the confession might be tainted (*HMA v McSwigan* (1937)).

Age of the suspect

It is clear that where the suspect is young, the courts are willing to apply less latitude to the police in considering whether a confession has been extracted unfairly. The age of the suspect was explicitly taken account of in *Codona v HMA* (1996), where the suspect was 14 years old. Other cases already dealt with in which the suspect was young include:

- *LB v HMA* (2003)—14-year-old tried for rape;
- *Hartley v HMA* (1979)—17-year-old on murder cha
- *Chalmers v HMA* (1954)—16-year-old charged witl
- *HMA v Aitken* (1926)—16-year-old on murder alleg
- *HMA v Rigg* (1946)—17-year-old on murder charge.

Although there are as yet no decided cases, there seems no reason in principle for an elderly suspect not to be able to rely on frailty or vulnerability caused by old age as a reason to argue that a confession has been provided in unfair circumstances.

Entrapment

Where a confession is extracted by way of entrapment, it may be regarded as having been extracted unfairly. In *HMA v Campbell* (1964), the trial judge (Lord Justice-Clerk Grant) sustained an objection to the admissibility of a confession in a murder case. The accused had telephoned a newspaper and had asked to meet with a reporter to provide information on a murder in exchange for payment. The newspaper agreed and a meeting was arranged in a public bar. The newspaper also contacted the police and a policeman, disguised as a reporter, attended the meeting with the reporter and the accused. During the meeting, the accused made an incriminating statement. He also handed over a pair of bloodstained trousers. The policeman took no active part in the meeting, he simply listened throughout. After the incriminating statement was made, he revealed his identity and cautioned the accused. The basis on which the statement was held to be inadmissible is contained in a short judgement— the accused should have been cautioned, given that the sole purpose of the presence of the policeman was to overhear the conversation.

Two cases in this area have involved entrapment by use of a hidden recording device. In the case of *Hopes v HMA* (1960), the charge was one of blackmail and the recorded conversation was transmitted to the witness (a police officer) at the same time as the conversation was taking place. The conversation was transmitted via a microphone on the complainer to a loud speaker and tape recorder in a nearby room where police officers were situated. The complainer was instructed by the police to arrange a meeting with the alleged blackmailer and it was at this meeting that the recording took place. The evidence of the conversation as recorded was held to be admissible; Lord Justice-General Clyde held that the means of recording was irrelevant. The evidence from the witness present would normally have been recorded by the use of the human mind. The use of tape as a medium of recording was no different in principle. The conclusions in this case were implicitly accepted when the direction to the jury by the trial judge in *Porter v HMA* (2005) were declared correct by the High Court.

A different result was obtained in the case of *HMA v Graham* (1991). There, a conversation was recorded by the use of a radio transmitter ncealed in the clothing of a businessman who was to have a business meeting with the accused. Although the meeting was to have taken place anyway, the police, on hearing of this, arranged the placing of the transmitter. Incriminating statements were made by the accused at the meeting and were recorded and transmitted to the police by use of the hidden equipment. Lord Cameron, the trial judge, accepted that the businessman was not "primed" with questions in advance. However, he knew of the nature of the police interest and, taking account of the content of the transcript of the conversation, it was clear that the businessman was not a disinterested party. In fact, Lord Cameron goes on to compare the situation with that where a third party is provided with a list of questions by the police to ask the suspect in the hope of securing an admission. Taking account of the circumstances, therefore, the court held that the absence of a caution was a fatal omission.

Where the entrapment is employed in order to catch the suspect in the act of committing the crime (as opposed to catching him make an incriminating statement), the evidence will generally be admissible, as long as the crime in question is one that would have been committed anyway. Entrapment in this sense has been defined as:

> "..when the state (in the form of the police or other agency) becomes involved in the instigation of crimes which would not otherwise be committed, whether by deception, pressure, encouragement or inducement." (*Brown v HMA* (2002) per Lord Philip).

This situation arose in *Weir v Jessop (No.2)* (1991). In this case, a police officer in plain clothes attended at the home of the accused and bought drugs from him, pretending to be a customer who had been sent there by the brother of the accused. The accused sold him drugs which were paid for with a marked banknote. A search warrant was then obtained and during the search, drugs were discovered at the accused's home.

The High Court on appeal held that the evidence uncovered following the operation was admissible. Key to the ruling of the court was the fact that the police had "applied no pressure, encouragement or inducement to incite the appellant to commit an offence that he would otherwise not have committed" (he would have sold the drugs had the officer been a genuine customer). The court went on to indicate that had the accused appeared reluctant to sell the drugs and the officer had pleaded with him to do so, that might have led to a different result. Also, if the accused had indicated that he was not in the habit of carrying out such transactions or that he had never sold drugs in this way, that too, may have affected the result in the case.

In considering the lack of a caution, the court made it clear that a caution was not required in order to warn a person that he should not commit an offence or that if he does so, he will be prosecuted for it. A caution concerns the situation in which a suspect might make an incriminating statement once suspicion has centred on him.

It has been made clear that there is no need to establish prejudice in order to succeed in an entrapment argument where the accused has been trapped into committing a crime he would not otherwise have committed. Lord Philip in *Brown v HMA* (2002) (with whom, on this point, Lord Clarke agreed), put it in this way:

> "In entrapment cases, the abuse of state power is so fundamentally unacceptable that it is not necessary to investigate whether the accused has been prejudiced or has been the victim of any form of unfairness. Indeed one can envisage cases of entrapment where it might be difficult to conclude that an accused had been truly (as opposed to theoretically) prejudiced or the victim of unfairness."

Article 8 of the ECHR may well play a role in such cases. All of the above authorities were pre-1998 cases, so it is not clear how persuasive they would be in the face of an Article 8 challenge.

One of the only vaguely relevant cases decided on the basis of Article 8 is not really comparable with those dealt with above. *Dudley v HMA* (2003), involved the recording of a prisoner's telephone call in which the prisoner and a friend discussed bringing some drugs to the prison. The friend was arrested on arrival and was found to be in possession of drugs. The court took the view that although the interception of the call and the passing of information about the call represented an intrusion into the accused's private life under Article 8(1), in terms of Article 8(2) this was permissible since it was in accordance with the law and necessary in a democratic society in the interests of the prevention of crime.

In *Gilchrist v HMA* (2004), a surveillance operation where undercover police officers viewed the handing over of a bag of drugs in a public street, was held not to breach the Article 8(1) right to respect for privacy.

The terms of the Regulation of Investigatory Powers (Scotland) Act 2000 may also be breached where a surveillance operation is carried out without, or not in accordance with, authorisation. It has been made clear that Article 8 plays a role in determining whether authorisation under the Act is obtained (see, for surveillance cases on the Act and Article 8, *Gilchrist v HMA* (2004); *Henderson and Marnoch v HMA* (2005)). The Interception of Communications Act 1985 is also relevant here, and should be complied with when it applies (see, for a surveillance case involving the Act, *Porter v HMA* (2005)).

Accidental overhearing

Where an incriminating statement is overheard without design, it is clear that it is admissible. In *Jamieson v Annan* (1988), two persons were in police custody in two cells situated close to one another. A police officer on duty overheard the beginning of an incriminating conversation being shouted between the two suspects. The officer immediately went to discuss the matter with a colleague and both returned to the area and listened to the remainder of the conversation. Objection was taken to the admissibility of the officers' evidence about what they overheard. The High Court upheld the sheriff's refusal of the objection and the evidence was held to be admissible. They indicated that there was no doubt that the evidence from the first officer about overhearing the initial part of the conversation was admissible as he had overheard it by accident. When he fetched his colleague, the officers had not acted improperly, the conversation between the suspects was entirely voluntary, and there was no suggestion of inducement.

Inducements or threats

We have seen how a suspect can be duped into providing an incriminating statement to the police, in circumstances where an undercover operation occurs. However, on some occasions an accused person might be offered a straightforward inducement, or might be threatened, in order to persuade him to offer a confession.

It is clear that there are no restrictions on the type of threat or inducement that might, if offered, prove fatal to the admissibility of a statement. Clearly a threat of violence will be, if established, sufficient to taint the statement. A threat of arrest and detention, even if only for a few nights, may be sufficient to render a statement inadmissible (*Black v Annan* (1995)). A threat of exposure of an adulterous relationship may also be sufficient (*Harley v HMA* (1996)).

It is important to note that where the Crown is seeking to introduce the statement, the burden remains on the Crown to satisfy the court that the statement is admissible. Even where the accused challenges the admissibility of the statement and is offering evidence of a threat or inducement, the burden remains on the Crown. Where that burden is inverted, this will be fatal to a conviction (*Black v Annan* (1995)).

It is also clear that the question is not one of the degree of inducement or threat used. Once it is accepted that there has been impropriety or pressurisation, the only question is whether or not what happened was, in all the circumstances, fair (*Black v Annan* (1995)).

It seems that there need not be a causal connection established between the threat or inducement and the provision of the statement (again, *Black v Annan* (1995)). While this might seem, at first sight, surprising such a link may be very difficult to establish and in any event the test is always one of fairness, not cause and effect.

Although most of the cases in this category deal with threats, it is clear that positive pressure in the form of an inducement can taint the admissibility of a statement. Obvious examples might include an offer of money, cigarettes, drugs, a visit from a partner, friend or relative, or of bail, while in custody. Once again, there is no limit to the circumstances in which a potential inducement might exist, the test always being one of fairness.

WITNESSES

Rules exist in order to regulate which persons are permitted to give evidence in criminal cases and whether they can, even if permitted to do so, be forced to give evidence.

There are two key concepts here:

1. Competency—this dictates whether a particular person is permitted, as a matter of law, to give evidence; and
2. Compellability—this concept is applied to discover if a particular witness who is competent can be forced, against his will, to give evidence.

The application of these concepts in the case of the vast majority of potential witnesses is not problematic. Most persons are permitted to give evidence and can be compelled to do so, even if they would rather not.

One situation that is relevant is not covered here, but is dealt with elsewhere. Sometimes a witness is competent, and in a general sense, compellable, but he may be permitted by the court to refuse to answer certain questions on the basis that the answer is protected by a recognised form of privilege. Privilege is dealt with elsewhere. Here we will concentrate on the compellability of a witness generally.

One further situation is where the witness is competent and compellable, but where he is classed as a vulnerable witness. This is dealt with below.

There are various categories of witness that are affected by competency and/or compellability considerations, and we will deal with each now. In doing so, some of the other aspects of these particular witness categories will be highlighted along the way.

Insane persons

Insanity is not an automatic bar to giving evidence, such witnesses are competent and compellable as long as they can tell the difference between truth and lies. Each case will be different and the judge will decide on whether the witness is fit to testify. In so deciding, he might hear evidence from experts as happened in *HMA v Stott* (1894). In that case, in directions to the jury, the judge commented on the weight to be attached to such evidence and he advised the jury that limited reliance should be placed on the testimony.

It is possible that such a witness will be categorised as a vulnerable witness (see later) and this will expose the witness to certain statutory measures providing for the method in which evidence can be given.

Witnesses with communication problems

Examples of these could include a speech impediment, stutter, being dumb or deaf and a heavy accent (foreign or domestic). An interpreter can be used, written answers given or sign language but credibility can be difficult to determine in these situations. If, at the end of the day, the witness is unintelligible, he will be deemed an incompetent witness.

Accused as a witness
The following general points can be made:

- The accused is a competent witness for the defence (s.266(1) of the 1995 Act). However, he is neither competent nor compellable as a prosecution witness.

- If the accused chooses not to give evidence, this can be commented upon by the court and used in weighing the evidence as a whole, however, the judge must be careful here when directing a jury. Lord Justice-General Normand in *Scott v HMA* (1946) indicated that such comments must be made with restraint and only where there are special circumstances that require them. Also, the weight given to this factor in the direction to the jury should not be distorted.

- The prosecutor can adversely comment on the accused's silence. The same situation applies with the comments by a judge in his direction to the jury (above).

- A co-accused can probably do likewise, although no direct Scottish authority exists on the point.

- An accused who chooses to give evidence can be asked questions which might incriminate him in relation to the offence charged (s.266(3) of the 1995 Act).

- Once an accused person ceases to be an accused, he is a compellable and competent witness for the Crown (s.266(10) of the 1995 Act). Therefore, if the accused pleads guilty to, or is acquitted of, all charges against him (or a mixture of the two) or if the case has been deserted (abandoned) by the prosecutor, he can become an ordinary witness against any other accused. Sometimes, a prosecutor will consider deserting a case against a co-accused in order to then call him as a witness against the remaining accused.

Co- accused as a witness
When two or more accused appear on the same complaint or indictment, they are said to be co-accused. They can appear on the same charges or on different charges in the same complaint or indictment, or a mixture of both.

There has to be some connection between the charges and the accused before the accused can appear on the complaint or indictment together and an accused person can apply to the court to be separated onto a different complaint/indictment, if he feels that he would be materially prejudiced by being a co-accused.

The following additional comments can be made on a co-accused as a witness:

- One accused can ask a co-accused who gives evidence any question in cross examination (s.266(9)(b) of the 1995 Act), or he can, irrespective of the defence being run, call a co-accused as a witness (s.266(9)(a) of the 1995 Act). This can only be done with his consent, since a co-accused is a competent witness for an accused but not a compellable one. However, he cannot do both (*i.e.* call the co-accused as a witness and then cross examine him when he gives evidence on own behalf).

- Where an accused gives evidence against a co-accused, he loses his protection from questions about his character or criminal record (dealt with elsewhere) and both the co-accused and the prosecutor can then attack the character of the accused.

- Although an accused person can be called to give evidence for a co-accused, if he agrees (which he has to (see above)), he probably cannot be compelled to incriminate himself. This is a reasonable implication from s.266(3) of the 1995 Act.

- Evidence from an accused can incriminate a co-accused in the same case (*Todd v HMA* (1984); 5 bench decision). Again, the rule in s.266(10) of the 1995 Act applies where the co-accused wishes to call a former accused as a witness (he is competent and compellable).

Accomplice as a witness

An accomplice is also known as a *socius criminis*. This special status goes to a witness who has already been convicted of the crime or who gives evidence on the basis that he is an accomplice (*Wallace v HMA* (1952)). This case has been partly superseded, as there are only two categories of accomplice now, not three, as stated in that case.

Such a witness, if specifically called by the Crown as an accomplice to give evidence, is immune from further prosecution *for the same offence*.

The rationale behind the immunity was explained by Lord Justice-General Clyde in *McGinley v McLeod* (1963) as follows:

> "[it is] designed to encourage [the accomplice] to tell the truth without fear of thereby incriminating himself and becoming liable to prosecution."

On the facts of that case (see below), it was held that the immunity did not apply, partly because the three accused were "antagonists mutually accusing each other" hence, were not genuine accomplices.

Where a Crown witness is giving evidence about a similar related matter, but not the precise matter covered in the libel (wording of the charge), the witness will not be immune from prosecution. This limitation was discussed in *McGinley v McLeod* (1963). The case arose out of a fight lasting for a short period in one street, and continuing shortly afterwards in a neighbouring street. Three persons were involved. The first accused was tried alone for assault and the other two accused gave evidence for the Crown against him. On the same day, the trial of the other two as co-accused with each other took place. They argued, following their conviction, that they were immune from prosecution having given evidence for the Crown in the trial of the first accused. Lord Justice-General Clyde, in rejecting the appeal, held that the two accused were not accomplices of the first accused, since the place of the offences in the two trials were different, those accused were different and the offences were different (in the first trial the assault allegation involved the use of a bottle, in the second trial, the charge was assault by kicking).

Another example is *O'Neill v Wilson* (1983). In that case, a police officer had gone to the home of an individual, who was a suspect in a crime. On arrival, there occurred a violent incident involving the police officer, the suspect (who was the householder) and another member of the family of the suspect. Following this incident, the householder and the family member were tried for assaulting the officer. The officer gave evidence for the Crown in that case, but both accused were acquitted. Thereafter, the officer was charged with assault and in his trial he argued that he was immune from prosecution since the crime alleged against him had occurred on the same occasion as the one for which he had been called as a Crown witness. It was held, however, that the crimes alleged, while taking place at the same time, were different crimes from each other so the immunity was held not to apply.

It is clear that a witness claiming immunity as an accomplice must have been called specifically as an accomplice. In *O'Neill v Wilson* (1983) (above), Lord Justice-General Emslie stated:

> "Unlike any other witness, the *socius criminis* is called by the Crown for the express purpose of testifying that he was an accomplice in the crime charged."

In that case, the appellant was not led in order to confess his involvement in the crime or in any crime, so the status did not attach to him for this reason, in addition to the reasons provided above. The approach in this case has been more recently affirmed in *Cochrane v HMA* (2002).

It should be noted that where the witness has not been accorded the status of an accomplice or has not been called as one, he still has the right to refuse to incriminate himself while giving evidence (dealt with elsewhere). If he is called as an accomplice, he does not have that right since he does not need it as he is immune from prosecution.

Spouse of the accused as a witness

Spouses of accused persons hold a special status in Scots law. The spouse of an accused is a *competent* witness *for* the accused, co-accused or prosecutor, *i.e.* everyone in a trial (s.264(1) of the 1995 Act). However, a person cannot be *compelled* to give evidence for the Crown or a co-accused *against* his or her spouse. A spouse is compellable only as a witness *for* the accused who is his or her spouse.

In *Hunter v HMA* (1984), the trial judge informed the wife of the accused (the accused had called her as a witness) that she need not answer any questions, and she declined to give evidence. In that case, the High Court held that the trial judge had erred in so informing her, but that this did not constitute a miscarriage of justice, so the appeal was refused. The court conducted an examination of the accused's claims of what the content of the wife's evidence would have been, had she not been misinformed by the judge. However, this account did not disclose any information that would, in the view of the High Court, have been useful in exculpation of the accused, hence the refusal of the appeal.

There is an exception to the rule. Where the spouse is the alleged victim of the accused's crime, the victim can be *compelled* by the Crown to give evidence. Usually, such cases involve allegations of violence by one spouse against another, but this is not always the case, *e.g. Foster v HMA* (1932) involved a charge of forgery.

The failure of the spouse to testify cannot be adversely commented upon by Crown or defence (but possibly by a judge); s.264(3) of the 1995 Act.

Also, once a spouse chooses to give evidence, he/she can only refuse to answer questions falling into two categories:

- Questions the answers to which might incriminate them.
- Questions which might result in a breach of the "marital communications" privilege (dealt with later).

Otherwise, all questions must be answered. In *Bates v* HMA (1989), the conviction was upheld despite the fact that a misdirection had been given to the witness. In that case, Lord Justice-Clerk Ross stated the rule in the following terms:

> "[the spouse should have been directed that] ...although she was entitled to give evidence, she could not be compelled to do so, but that, if she did give evidence, she would require to answer all questions put to her."

Judges

In their non-official capacity, judges are treated like any other witness. In their official capacity, they can be witnesses to anything that happens in the court room, such as a disturbance. A judge can also be called as a witness to disclose the details of any evidence led before him. The most common such instance is in a perjury (lying on oath) trial of a witness. For an example see *Davidson v McFadyean* (1942).

Prosecutors

A prosecutor is also treated in the same way as any other witness, except that he cannot be a witness in a case he is presenting. This was confirmed, albeit on an *obiter* basis, in *Mackintosh v Wooster* (1919).

Although not legally required, it is regarded as good practice for the prosecutor concerned to have nothing to do with the preparation of the case (see the comments of Lord Deas to this effect in *Ferguson v Webster* (1869)). Although such a situation would not necessarily represent a bar to the prosecutor giving evidence, it might be a breach of the accused's right to a fair trial under Article 6 of the ECHR, since the witness would have access to information in his role as a prosecutor that other witnesses and the accused would not have access to.

Defence solicitor

An accused person has the right to call his solicitor (even the solicitor conducting the case in court) as a witness (s.265 of the 1995 Act). In *Campbell v Cochrane* (1928), the accused's agent who had been conducting the trial for the whole of the Crown case, sought to give evidence, and the trial judge upheld an objection to this. The High Court allowed the subsequent appeal, stating that the course of action proposed was perfectly competent, and that the rule regarding the presence in court of a later witness during earlier evidence (see below), does not apply when the witness who has been present is the agent conducting the case.

It should be noted, however, that the solicitor-client privilege (dealt with elsewhere) cannot then be relied upon (s.265(2) of the 1995 Act).

Heads of State

The monarch is probably competent but not compellable. Other members of the royal family are both. In addition, by s.20 of the State Immunity Act 1978, foreign heads of state, their families and domestic staff are competent but not compellable.

Diplomats and consular officials

According to the Diplomatic Privileges Act 1964 (which incorporates into UK law the provisions of the Vienna Convention on Diplomatic Relations (Cmnd 2565)), the head of a diplomatic mission based in the UK and his staff are competent but not compellable. The same follows for their families. However, consular officials who are part-time are competent and compellable although full time officials are not compellable.

Bankers

A bank official is competent but not compellable in criminal proceedings in matters relating to entries in the bank's books, unless by order of a judge for special cause (Bankers Books Evidence Act 1879, s.6). However, where a party wishes to put a copy of an entry to a banker to confirm that it is a true copy, he will be competent and compellable for this purpose (1879 Act, s.5).

Previous attendees in court
Where a witness has heard evidence before giving evidence himself, if permission has not been obtained for him to sit in court beforehand, the court has discretion to overlook his earlier presence and allow him to give evidence (s.267(2) of the 1995 Act). This power to excuse the situation is only exercisable where:

- no culpable negligence or criminal intent is involved; and
- the witness is not unduly instructed or influenced by what he has heard; and
- no injustice would result.

The usual course is to ask for advance permission for the attendance of the witness. Under s.267(1) of the 1995 Act, such permission can only be granted if to do so would be in the interests of justice. However, if the witness is an expert, unless there is an objection, he will be allowed to sit in on factual evidence, but not evidence of another expert (unless an application is made). The factual background might be relevant to the opinion of the expert, so this is often an important facility.

The accused may testify, despite his presence throughout the trial, as may the accused's agent—see *Campbell v Cochrane* (1928) on the latter.

Vulnerable witnesses
The law in this area is undergoing a major revisal. The Vulnerable Witnesses (Scotland) Act 2004 is partly in force at the time of writing and will be phased in over a period of a few years. In the meantime, for some cases, the pre-2004 Act regime still applies, therefore, both regimes will be considered. The provisions in Part 1 of the 2004 Act affect criminal cases only. Those in Part 2 apply to civil cases. The timetable for the implementation of the 2004 Act in criminal cases is, at the time of writing, as follows:

Phase 1—Main provisions in force from April 1, 2005

- Section 1 (introducing special measures for the giving of evidence) in High Court and solemn sheriff court proceedings and for child witnesses only;
- Section 2 (notice provisions for special measures) on the same basis as s.1;
- Section 6 (accused prohibited from conducting defence in certain cases involving child witnesses under the age of 12) in High Court and solemn sheriff court proceedings;

- Section 24 (abolition of the competency test) for all criminal cases.

Phase 2—April 2006
From this date, it is planned that the provisions of the Act relating to adult vulnerable witnesses will apply, but only in solemn sheriff court and in High Court cases.

Phase 3—2007
During 2007, all of the provisions for child and adult vulnerable witnesses will be extended to sheriff court summary cases.

There are two main aspects of specialty to consider:

1. The competency of a child witness.
2. Measures to take evidence of a child.

The competency of a child witness
Although from April 1, 2005 the competency test has been abolished for all criminal cases, as explained below, the test as developed before 2004 may still be relevant.

Pre-2004 Act (pre-April 1, 2005)
There is no lower age limit for a child witness, and in theory a child of any age might be a competent witness. Some examples of cases in which this has been an issue are:

- *Millar* (1870)—three-year-old testified in sexual assault case (had made a *de recenti* statement).
- *Thomson* (1857)—three-year-old not allowed to testify in murder case (no *res gestae* statement).

The competency test was twofold; whether the child is able to (1) understand the concept of telling the truth, and (2) understand the duty to tell the truth.

The task of testing these matters is that of the judge and he can hear evidence on this if he wishes.

Dealing with the first test, the judge must test the ability of the witness to understand the truth. He does this by establishing if the witness understands the difference between truth and lies. However, getting an affirmative answer from the child on this is not enough. The practice involves a "preliminary interrogation" of the child, to actively test the child's ability to understand the difference. A popular method involves the placing of obvious questions to the child. The level of these questions will depend on the age of the child.

At the second stage, the judge must tell the child that he should tell the truth. Some guidelines were confirmed by Lord Justice-General Hope in *Quinn v Lees* (1994):

- an admonishment to tell the truth if the child is under 12;
- a full oath should be administered if over 14;
- age 12–14—will depend on whether the judge is satisfied that the child will understand the oath.

In some cases the courts have examined these requirements very closely. For example, in *Rees v Lowe* (1989), it was held that the sheriff did not go far enough when he told the witness that she should answer the questions as best as she could. There was no attempt to carry out a preliminary examination and no admonishment to tell the truth was given. The witness was three years old. The conviction was, as a result, quashed. In the less obvious case of *Kelly v Docherty* (1991), a seven-year-old witness was asked by the sheriff if he would tell the truth and the witness agreed that he would. However, the sheriff failed to conduct a preliminary examination of the child. The sheriff pointed out that he carried out a continuous assessment of the competency of the witness and the longer the evidence was given, the more convinced he became that the child was telling the truth. However, this was regarded as inadequate and once again the conviction was quashed. In *Quinn v Lees* (1994), it was held on appeal that the sheriff had followed the correct procedure.

The question of whether the court should hear extrinsic evidence on the issue of the child's ability to tell the truth is undecided. In *P v HMA* (1991), the court seems to assume that such evidence is competent, although not required in that case. In *HMA v Grimmond* (2001), it was held that such evidence is not permitted where the witness does not suffer from mental illness. The former view is probably correct, given the relaxation in recent cases of the types of expert behavioural witness who can give evidence—see the discussion of these cases in the section on opinion evidence in part 2, above. Although these are not cases in which there was a child competency question, they are indirectly relevant.

It should also be noted that these tests and any evidence on them were, before April 2005, conducted in advance of the child witness giving evidence.

Post-April 1, 2005

The Vulnerable Witnesses (Scotland) Act 2004, abolishes the competence test altogether. Section 24 provides:

> "s.24(1) The evidence of any person called as a witness (referred to in this section as "the witness") in criminal or civil proceedings is not inadmissible solely because the witness does not understand—
>
> (a) the nature of the duty of a witness to give truthful evidence, or

(b) the difference between truth and lies.

(2) Accordingly, the court must not, at any time before the witness gives evidence, take any step intended to establish whether the witness understands those matters."

It is not clear how this section will operate. It seems that the court cannot exclude such evidence in advance of the witness beginning testimony unless it can do so on another ground. This seems odd, since it means that a witness who has no understanding of the difference between truth or lies and/or has no understanding of the nature of the duty to tell the truth, must still be allowed to give evidence. However, the opponent of the party leading that witness might cross-examine the witness to demonstrate these matters, and in theory presumably little or no weight in such cases will be placed on the evidence of the witness. Also, the court is only prohibited from seeking to ascertain the competency of the child witness "at any time before the witness gives evidence". Consequently, if a judge becomes concerned after a witness begins his evidence that the witness does not understand either matter, one possible interpretation of the section would allow the tests to be applied at that time. A decision could then be made, on the basis that the tests are not satisfied, that the remaining evidence of the witness is inadmissible. If such a determination can be made during the evidence, the pre-2004 case law will still be applicable.

In addition, it would seem that the case law on the admonishment will still be useful post-2004 since the judge must decide how the duty to tell the truth is conveyed to the witness (oath or admonition) as distinct from establishing that the witness understands that duty (the latter of which is excluded by s. 24(1)(a)).

No doubt the abolition in s.24 will come under scrutiny from an ECHR Article 6 compatibility perspective in the near future.

Measures to take evidence from a child

Assuming a child is a competent witness, the question of how his evidence should be taken arises. It is recognised that in any case, special measures should be taken by the court to make the experience for a child witness easier and more reliable (more likely to extract the truth). This need is even more acute where the witness is likely to be distressed, *e.g.* where the child is the victim of an alleged crime. However, the judge can, with the best of intentions, take matters too far—see *McKie v HMA* (1997), where the High Court criticised the sheriff for intervening to comfort a child witness when a carer was available to do so.

Since at the time of writing the special measures in the 2004 Act are only in force in relation to child witnesses in solemn cases, both the pre and post-2004 Act positions will be dealt with.

Pre-2004 Act

The following devices exist to make the task of giving evidence easier for a child:

- the Lord Justice-General's *Memorandum on Child Witnesses*, July 1990—this is advice on how, from a practical point of view, a judge can put a child witness at ease;
- the enactment of s.271 of the 1995 Act and case law on that section—see below;
- s.259 of 1995 Act on hearsay evidence—we have seen how the use of a hearsay statement (for example, a statement given to a social worker) can be used in order to prevent the child having to give evidence at all;
- s.45 of the Children and Young Persons Act 1937—the court can be cleared (emptied) where a case involves allegations of indecent and immoral conduct where a child under 16 years old is to give evidence.

1995 Act, s.271

This section provides for the following measures:

- evidence of a child taken out of court by a Commissioner and recorded by videotape;
- evidence of child by live TV link;
- screen to conceal the witness while giving evidence;
- sheriff can transfer the case to another court if equipment not available;
- identification evidence can be relayed through a third party.

There have been a number of cases on TV link evidence under s.271 (or under the predecessor to that section, s.56 of the Law Reform (Miscellaneous Provisions) (Scotland) Act 1990). See *HMA v Birkett* (1992), an application for one of five children granted under the 1990 Act and followed in *HMA v McGrattan* (1996), this time under s.271. Finally, in *Brotherston v HMA* (1995), again a case under s.56 of the 1990 Act, the value of evidence by TV link was commented on by Lord Justice General Hope.

Measures to take evidence from a vulnerable adult

Keeping with the pre-2004 Act position, the s.271 facilities for the taking of evidence apply to three categories of vulnerable witness. The first is a child (person under the age of 16). The other two categories are as follows:

- witnesses suffering from a mental disorder in terms of the mental health legislation—expert evidence would be needed here; and

- witnesses who appear to the court to suffer from "significant impairment of intelligence and social functioning"—expert evidence will probably be needed here also.

Measures to take evidence from a vulnerable witness— the post-2004 Act position

The 2004 Act provides that s.271 of the 1995 Act is to be replaced with new provisions. These involve three new categories of vulnerable witness:

- a child under 16 at the date of commencement of proceedings;
- an adult with a mental disorder where there is a significant risk that the quality of evidence to be given will be diminished by that disorder; and
- an adult with no such disorder but where there is a significant risk that the quality of evidence to be given will be diminished due to fear or distress associated with the giving of evidence.

Certain factors require to be taken into account by the court in determining whether or not a person is a vulnerable witness (new s.271 (2) of the 1995 Act).

The following other features are relevant:

- the special measures available consist of live TV link; screen; evidence on commission; the use of "supporters" and the use of a prior statement as evidence in chief (s.1 of the 2004 Act, inserting new s.271H–271M into the 1995 Act);
- advance notice provisions are now in place (s.2 of the 2004 Act, amending various provisions of the 1995 Act);
- the court has no discretion where the witness is a child and a TV link or screen is sought (known as "standard special measures"); otherwise it can refuse application (s.1 of the 2004 Act adding a new s.271A(5)(a)(i) and (14));
- can be used by prosecution or defence—the accused can be a "vulnerable witness".

It remains to be seen how these provisions will operate. Perhaps the most significant changes are the advance notification provisions and the new category of vulnerable witness, namely those who are vulnerable due to fear or distress associated with the giving of evidence. Also, any mental disorder would now have to affect the likely quality of the evidence, while under the earlier provisions, a mental disorder in itself would be enough. The case law on screens from previous legislation will still be relevant. In fact, it seems possible to seek the use of a witness screen at common law if the 1995 Act is inapplicable (*Hampson v HMA* (2003)).

Also relevant, even after the application of the 2004 Act, is the Lord Justice-General's *Memorandum on Child Witnesses*, July 1990, which holds relevance for both criminal and civil cases.

PRESUMPTIONS

Only four of the main presumptions are exclusively applicable in criminal cases. These are:

- The presumption of innocence;
- The presumption of recent possession of stolen goods;
- The presumption of nonage as a bar to a criminal trial;
- The presumption of lack of sexual consent by a female under 12.

All other presumptions are primarily applicable in civil cases. These other presumptions are dealt with in the section on civil evidence. The categories of types of presumption are explained in Part 1. We will now turn to the four, exclusively criminal, presumptions.

Presumption of innocence

For centuries, it has been accepted that the accused in a criminal trial is presumed to be innocent. This is linked into the placing of the burden of proof in all criminal cases on the Crown. The accused is presumed to be innocent unless the Crown proves otherwise. A further consequence of the interaction between the presumption of innocence and the burden of proof in criminal cases is the right to silence of the accused, both when being interviewed by the police (note the terms of the common law caution, dealt with elsewhere) and in court (the accused is not a competent or compellable witness for the Crown—dealt with elsewhere). On the right to silence generally see *Robertson v Maxwell* (1951).

This presumption has recently been enshrined in statute following the enactment of the Human Rights Act 1998. Article 6(2) of the ECHR contains such a right, and this part of Article 6 has spawned some major cases, including *R v Lambert* (2001) and *Mackintosh, Petitioner* (2001), both referred to under 'burden of proof' (above).

This presumption qualifies as an irrebuttable presumption of law.

Recent possession of stolen goods

This is also dealt with elsewhere. It is classed as a presumption because once the elements identified in *Fox v Patterson* (1948) have been established by the Crown, it is presumed that the accused is guilty and he must provide an innocent explanation. This type of case is sometimes described as an example of the reversal of the burden of proof.

This is an example of a rebuttable presumption of fact.

Nonage as a bar to criminal trial

Section 41 of the Criminal Procedure (Scotland) Act 1995 is a short section which provides:

> "It shall be conclusively presumed that no child under the age of eight years can be guilty of any offence."

A child under eight is deemed not to be capable of possessing the *mens rea* necessary to commit an offence.

This is an irrebuttable presumption of law.

Lack of sexual consent of a female under 12

A female who is under 12 years old is deemed incapable of giving consent to sexual intercourse. This is a common law presumption and the practical application of it is that any sexual intercourse between a male and a female, where the latter is under the age of 12, is technically rape, whether or not the female in fact consented. However, there are alternative charges available to a prosecutor in such a situation and the charge need not always be one of rape. Under the Criminal Law (Consolidation) (Scotland) Act 1995, s.5(2), there is an alternative charge of sexual intercourse with a girl under 13, which is available in certain circumstances.

PRIVILEGE

Sometimes where evidence from a witness is admissible and the witness is competent and compellable, the witness can refuse to answer certain questions or can refuse to produce certain documents as he is said to have the "privilege" of not answering. This category of situation is more apparent in civil than in criminal cases. There are three main situations in which privilege exists in criminal cases, the first of which is fundamental:

- privilege against self-incrimination;
- marital communications privilege;
- legal adviser-client privilege.

We will deal with the first two here. The third applies on equal terms in both civil and criminal cases, and is dealt with in Part 4 of this book.

Self-incrimination privilege—accused

The position of the accused alone will be dealt with here, the application of this privilege to all other witnesses will be dealt within part 4.

This fundamental principle has been accepted by Scots law for some time. In the case of *Livingstone v Murray* (1830), it was described as an "inviolable principle".

The principle, as far as evidence of the accused during a trial is concerned, only applies to allow the accused to remain silent. The accused does not have to give evidence at his trial, although, if he chooses to do so, the privilege flies off (but only for the crime in question). Neither can the accused be forced to incriminate himself for some other crime (s.266(4) of the 1995 Act), unless certain conditions apply (see above under character of the accused for these conditions). For present purposes, it should be noted that the privilege, to this extent, carries statutory protection.

The rule allows the question to be put to the accused and only prevents the answer being given. However, the accused is not expected to refuse to answer in such a situation without guidance and so the judge has a role in advising the witness of the privilege. Lord President Inglis in *Kirkwood v Kirkwood* (1875) indicated that normally the judge will be very careful to warn the witness. One of the agents can intervene to ask the judge to issue a warning or it can be given before evidence begins.

The principle is affirmed by the terms of Article 6 of the ECHR as part of the right to a fair trial. Although it does not contain a specific right not to incriminate, it has been inferred. In *Saunders v UK* (1996), the European Court of Human Rights stated:

> "...the right not to incriminate oneself, like the right to silence, was a generally recognised international standard which lay at the heart of the notion of a fair procedure [under Article 6]."

As far as the accused is concerned, the right not to self-incriminate has had most significance in the context of extra judicial (out of court) statements or confessions and has been tested in two major ECHR decisions:

- *Saunders v UK* (1996)—the accused was forced to answer questions—breach of privilege;
- *Brown v Stott* (2001)—s.172 of the Road Traffic Act 1988—although not breach of Article 6, the accused was forced under pain of prosecution to answer—but held by the Privy Council (overturning the High Court on a devolution issue) that this was legitimate given the aim of the provision and the public interest.

Marital communications privilege

This is contained, for criminal cases, in s.264(2)(b) of the 1995 Act which states "nothing shall compel a spouse to disclose any communication made between the spouses during the marriage". There is no definition of communication and it could be written or oral. Although there is no direct authority on this, it seems that the privilege ends with divorce (but not separation). It only applies to married couples. The rationale for the privilege is the preservation of the sanctity of marriage.

PART 4. THE LAW OF EVIDENCE IN CIVIL CASES

BURDEN OF PROOF

In order to determine which party bears the burden on which issue, there is a simple rule. Where a party affirmatively relies upon a fact and where it is essential to the establishment of his case, he will bear the legal burden of proving that fact. If he fails to prove it (fails to discharge the burden), it will be deemed not to have been established and he will lose his case. The following statements are also true of the burden in a civil case:

- the evidential and persuasive burdens rest on the party who would lose on the issue if no other evidence was led, or if at the end of the case the evidence led by both on the issue is equally persuasive;
- the party who raises the issue must prove it;
- the other party needs to prove nothing on any issue relied upon by his opponent.

Of course, this means that the main burden will usually lie on the pursuer. However, where the defender asserts a positive defence (not just a denial of his opponent's case) he will bear the legal burden of establishing that defence.

Sometimes the court intervenes where it is not clear upon which party a particular burden lies. In such cases, the courts apply a general rule that a party should not be required to prove a negative, and that the party who would require to prove a positive fact if the burden were to be borne by him, will be the party to bear the burden. This is done on the basis that it is generally easier to prove a positive than a negative (see, *e.g.* the English case of *Constantine Steamship Line v Imperial Smelting Corp Ltd* (1942)).

The question of whether an expert for a defender in a personal injury action requires to outline any alternative explanations for the cause of an injury, not consistent with liability, in order to negate a claim, was discussed in the Scottish House of Lords case of *Thomson v Kvaerner Govan Ltd* (2004). The House of Lords, by a majority of 4–1, found that the reliance placed upon the inability of the defender's expert to devise an alternative explanation effectively involved inverting the burden of proof. The defenders had no obligation to prove anything, except in the special case of *res ipsa loquitur*, which required a reasonable inference of negligence on the part of the defenders in the first place (see later on this).

The pursuer bore the burden of proving that the plank in question broke, injuring him, in circumstances demonstrating negligence on the part of the defenders. The fact that the defence expert discredited this explanation did not mean that he had to come up with an alternative explanation himself.

It seems that this reasoning is correct, since defenders cannot be seen to be being punished for failing to produce their own theory as to how the accident happened in circumstances negating negligence on their part. They require solely to attack the account of the pursuer. Where they do so successfully, they win the case. To put it another way, the court does not require to find out what *did* happen; instead, it only decides if the pursuer has established that the defenders are to blame.

A number of other points should be noted on the burden of proof in civil cases:

- Sometimes a party will bear a burden to prove a negative, *e.g.* in a damages claim following a road traffic accident, the defender might aver that the pursuer did not take reasonable care for his own safety, but the onus will require some positive evidence, *e.g.* that the pursuer did not look both ways before crossing the road.
- The pursuer normally runs his case before the defender but sometimes the defender will be allowed to go first. If the order is altered, this does not alter where the burdens lie, simply the order in which they are discharged.
- A presumption, when relied upon, does not alter the burden from one party to another, it is simply a way in which the burden can be discharged. If rebuttable, the other party can lead evidence against it. However, the burden will still be on the first party.

Inversion of statutory burden

Sometimes a statute will reverse the burden of proof either expressly or by implication. An example of the former is under the Bills of Exchange Act 1882, s.30(1) which provides that "Every party whose signature appears on a bill is prima facie deemed to have become a party thereto for value".

However, the burden of proof can be "shifted" if it is established or admitted that the acceptance, issue or subsequent negotiation of the bill is affected with fraud, duress, force and fear or illegality (s.30(2)).

One main example of the inversion of the burden by implication is where the court has to be satisfied of something. There, the onus is on the party who has to so satisfy. For example, in *Kerrigan v Nelson* (1946), a repossession action in connection with rented property, the applicable legislation required the court to consider whether the granting of a repossession order would cause more hardship than not granting it. The Inner House agreed with the sheriff that where the tenant was seeking to establish that hardship would be caused by the granting of the order, the onus of satisfying the court of this was on the tenant, even though the landlord was seeking the court order.

Statutory qualification

Where a statute attaches a qualification to a particular statement, sometimes this can lead to the burden altering slightly. For example, *Nimmo v Alexander Cowan & Sons* (1967) was a case under the Factories Act 1961 s.29(1), which provided that the workplace is to be kept safe "so far as is reasonably practicable". It was held that the pursuer had to prove that the workplace was not safe in general terms and thereafter the onus to establish that precautions were taken (that the defender (employer) had done all that was reasonably practicable) fell on the defender. The reason for this is that, as Lord Guest put it, the relevant question would "be peculiarly within the employer's province".

Splitting of burden

Sometimes the persuasive and evidential burdens fall on different parties. This is exceptional and applies only where a fact lies peculiarly within the knowledge of one party. An example is the *Nimmo* case, above. Another example is the case of *McClure,Naismith, Brodie and Macfarlane v Stewart* (1887).

STANDARD OF PROOF

The standard of proof in civil cases in Scotland is that the essential facts must be established on *the balance of probabilities* (not beyond reasonable doubt—this is the criminal standard).

What does "the balance of probabilities" mean? A number of cases have attempted to define this concept. Lord Denning in *Miller v Minister of Pensions* (1947) put it in this way:

> "If the evidence is such that the tribunal can say 'we think it more probable than not', the burden is discharged- but if the probabilities are equal it is not."

It should be noted that Lord Denning is referring here to each essential factual issue (for example, was there a contract? was there foreseeability?) on which the party bears the burden of proof.

Another definition is provided by Lord Simon in the case of *Davies v Taylor* (1974):

> "...proof on a balance of probabilities [is] the burden of showing odds of at least 51 to 49 that such-and-such has taken place or will do so....in other words, is it more likely than not? ...If a possibility is conceivable but fanciful, the law disregards it entirely."

This could mean that various possible explanations are put for a particular occurrence and the court might reject them all as improbable, leaving the party bearing the burden of proof to lose the case. This happened in *Rhesa Shipping Co SA v Edmunds (The Popi M)* (1985).

Finally, it should be noted that the standard of proof in certain cases in which there is a criminal or non-civil element is on the balance of probabilities. These include:

- a civil action where there is an allegation of a crime (*Mullan v Anderson (No.1)* (1993); *Hastie v Hastie* (1985) (divorce));
- fatal accident inquiries (Fatal Accidents and Sudden Deaths Inquiry (Scotland) Act 1976 s.4(7));
- children's hearing referrals (except those under the Children (Scotland) Act 1995, s.52(2)(g), in which the standard is the criminal one);
- breach of interdict (*Morrow v Neil* (1975));
- breach of ECHR Article 3 (inhuman or degrading treatment) (*Napier v Scottish Ministers* (2005)).

SUFFICIENCY

Sufficiency generally

A concept related to the burden of proof is sufficiency. It is stated above that the burden on a party is to prove those facts essential to his case. The essential facts will vary from case to case. In a breach of contract case, these might be the essential facts for the pursuer:

1. The existence of a contract.
2. The failure to deliver goods under the contract.
3. The breach of a term of that contract as a result of the failure to deliver the goods.
4. The loss caused as a result of failure to deliver the goods.

If he fails to discharge the burden of proof on any of these issues, his case fails. In the same case, the defender might mount a defence that there was no valid contract since his agreement was induced by a negligent misrepresentation by the pursuer. In such a case he would bear the burden of proving these essential facts:

1. That a representation was made.
2. That it induced the defender into entering the contract.
3. That it was made by someone who had a duty to provide advice.

You will notice that these cases overlap. The pursuer will, in trying to establish point 1, above, be met by the defence of misrepresentation. The court is considering the burdens on both parties at the same time. It will be seen, therefore, that the operation of burdens is not always clear in practice. However, for the purposes of examining how the burden operates, the obligations should be separated out. In the example above, the court would consider under the pursuer's point 1, whether the basics of a contract had been met (offer, acceptance and intention to create legal relations). If satisfied on that, the attention would then shift to the defender to see if the defence of misrepresentation had been made out. If the pursuer fails on point 1, the case is over and the defender has won. If he succeeds on point 1, but the defender fails to establish his defence, the pursuer still requires to establish the remaining essential facts. His case may therefore still fail. Of course, all of this is going on at the same time, but in reality, the burdens play a part.

In delict cases, the dynamics would be the same. The essential facts would depend upon the delict involved. Thus, for a straight action of negligence, the elements of the "delict model" would require to be established by the pursuer (duty of care, breach of duty, causation and damage not too remote). On the other hand, if the action was for damages for economic loss, the main essential fact might be to establish that the loss is of a recoverable kind.

In reality, certain of the facts might be agreed, so in the contract example above, the only issue between the parties might be the level of damages where there is agreement that the contract is breached. In such a case, while the plaintiff still technically bears the burden of proving the facts, those facts will be agreed on paper before the evidence is led so that the evidence will focus only on the disputed area.

The final point is that in any particular case, the defender may bear no burden of proof at all. This will be the case where there are no essential facts for him to prove. This occurs where he is not mounting a specific defence, but is simply attacking the case of the pursuer. That is not to say that he will be leading no evidence. He may well be producing evidence, documentary and/or oral in his attempt to counter the pursuer's case. On the other hand, he may produce no evidence at all and simply sit back and say nothing. He might still win the case since the burden on the pursuer of proving his essential facts will exist, and must be discharged by him in order that he wins the case.

Abolition of corroboration

The Civil Evidence (Scotland) Act 1988, s.1 abolished the requirement to lead corroborated evidence in a civil case. Corroboration was a requirement prior to 1988 for personal injury actions and prior to 1968 for all civil actions. Corroborated evidence is evidence from at least two sources on the essential facts of the case.

Following the removal of the requirement for corroboration in 1968 for personal injury cases (the Law Reform (Miscellaneous Provisions) (Scotland) Act 1968, s.9), the courts seemed reluctant to let the need for corroboration go. Consequently, in *Morrison v Kelly* (1970), the Inner House suggested that where corroboration was available, it had to be produced. This seemed to fly in the face of the clear wording of the legislation (s.9 was worded very similarly to s.1 of the 1988 Act). However, the courts have more recently moved away from this idea. For example, in *Thomson v Tough Ropes* (1978), the judge accepted the evidence of the pursuer as to how the accident at work had happened. However, he found the only other witness for the pursuer, her work colleague who witnessed the incident, to be unreliable. The pursuer won the case and was awarded damages. This is a logical decision since there was one credible witness who gave an account of the incident which was consistent with liability. The fact that the same account was given by another, disbelieved witness (the pursuer's work colleague) is irrelevant. This case demonstrates that corroboration is not required in a civil case. Even where a corroborative witness is available but is not produced, this is not fatal in a civil case (*McCallum v British Railways Board* (1991); *Airnes v Chief Constable of Strathclyde* (1998)). However, the failure to do so might contribute to the court's view that the standard of proof has not been satisfied (*Gordon v Grampian Health Board* (1991)). Of course, in practice, a party will rarely fail to produce corroborative evidence where it is available, since it will strengthen the case before the court.

The abolition of the corroboration requirement in civil cases, coupled with a widely worded hearsay rule (see below), means that a case can be established on only one source of hearsay evidence. For an example of this see *K v Kennedy* (1992). In fact, in that case the principal source of the statement (a child) had given evidence which involved the retraction of that witness's earlier statement. The sheriff rejected her oral evidence and relied solely upon her (by now retracted) hearsay statement.

Exception to abolition—consistorial cases

Under the Civil Evidence (Scotland) Act 1988, s.8(2), even in undefended cases (*i.e.* where there is no response by the defender within the time limit, which would normally lead to decree in absence being granted), evidence will be needed in order for a decree to be granted. These cases include: divorce, separation and declarator of nullity of marriage. In such cases, s.8(3) goes on to provide that the requisite evidence shall "consist of or include evidence other than that of a party to the marriage", *i.e.* corroboration from a source other than the other party to the marriage. In these cases, evidence by affidavits (sworn statements) is usually provided, not oral evidence. The basis of such a rule in only these specific cases is the reluctance of the courts to break up a marriage.

However, this rule does not apply in two and five year separation "simplified" divorces.

In addition, something akin to the (criminal) *Moorov* doctrine applies, and this usually operates in adultery cases to link together more than one alleged act of adultery (*Whyte v Whyte* (1884); but not in *Michlek v Michlek* (1971)—5 year gap too long).

ADMISSIBILITY

Relevancy

In order for evidence in a civil case to be admissible it must be logically relevant to the issues in dispute. This may seem obvious, and it usually is. The general test of relevance has been referred to in Part 3, but is worth repeating here:

> " ...the ultimate test is whether the material in question has a reasonably direct bearing on the subject under investigation" (Lord Osborne in *Strathmore Group Ltd v Credit Lyonnais* (1994)).

The application of the basic test is not obvious in all cases. For example, in *Taylor v Taylor* (2000), an appeal in the Inner House in a divorce action, a question of relevancy arose in the context of questioning on matters of religious belief. The sheriff indicated that the court could only deal with law, and could not make a ruling on spiritual or religious matters and his approach was supported by the Inner House. The US case of *Knapp v The State* (1907) (discussed by *Sheldon*, pp.3–4) is a very interesting example of a court dealing with a genuine issue of relevance.

Such cases will be rare. However, there is one area in which the court may have to closely consider relevancy—where there is an issue of collateral evidence.

Collateral evidence

This is also often known as "similar fact" evidence and consists of evidence not directly related to the issues, but where something similar has occurred in the past. The party seeking to lead such evidence will usually be seeking to establish that conduct in the past by the other party in a similar situation is good evidence of what is likely to have happened on the occasion in question. We have seen how such matters are generally inadmissible in criminal cases. A similar approach is taken in civil cases, although the position here is not particularly clear.

From some early cases, it seemed clear that such evidence was inadmissible as irrelevant to the issues in dispute. For example, in *A v B* (1895), the pursuer was suing for damages, having allegedly been raped by the defender. The pursuer sought to introduce evidence suggesting that the defender had raped two other women. The evidence was disallowed on the ground that it was collateral. In the course of the case, Lord President Robertson said this:

> "Experience shows that it is better to sacrifice the aid which may be got from the more or less uncertain solution of collateral issues, than to spend a great amount of time, and confuse the jury [or court] with what, in the end, even supposing it to be certain, has only an indirect bearing on the matter in hand." (see also the case of *H v P* (1905), on allegations of prior acts of adultery).

On the other hand, similar fact evidence has been admitted in later Scottish civil cases. For example, in the case of *W Alexander & Sons v Dundee Corporation* (1950), the pursuer bus company sought to introduce evidence of previous occasions on which their buses had slid on the stretch of road the accident in question had occurred. The aim was to establish that the road was in a slippery condition as the materials used by the defenders (local authority) in constructing the road had melted and the road became slippery. The evidence was allowed and in allowing it, Lord Justice-Clerk Thomson said this:

> "..if it is established that the skidding of these vehicles on these other occasions was truly due to the condition of the road, then it seems to me that that is not a collateral issue at all but something having a direct bearing on the decision of the present case...There no doubt comes a point at which it is possible to say that the bearing of some fact is too indirect and too remote properly to assist the Court in deciding what the cause of the accident is; but I am quite clear that that point is far from being reached [in this case]."

Another civil case in which similar fact evidence was allowed is *Knutzen v Mauritzen* (1918), where the condition of meat delivered was in dispute and where the pursuers sought to adduce evidence from another customer of the defenders who had received meat in a similar poor state from the same consignment of the defenders' supply. This evidence was allowed as having a direct bearing on the facts in issue.

In consistorial cases, such as divorce actions, where, as an exception to the usual rule against the need for corroboration in civil cases, corroborative evidence is required from outwith the parties to the marriage (see earlier on this) collateral evidence has been allowed. For example, *Whyte v Whyte* (1884) was a divorce case involving an allegation by the pursuer of her husband's adultery. He was a minister. Evidence of an adulterous relationship with someone other than the named mistress was allowed due to the similarity of the allegation with the one concerning the named adulterer. Both relationships were between the minister and domestic servants, and in both, adultery was alleged to have been committed in the manse. In fact, something akin to the *Moorov* doctrine in criminal cases is applied here, so time lapse between the incidents is taken account of (see also *Michlek v Michlek* (1971)).

The question of whether evidence outwith the four corners of the case will be regarded as collateral and therefore irrelevant, or whether it will be treated as of direct relevance to the issues in dispute, will depend on the facts of the case. It seems that in civil cases, the courts are more relaxed about admitting such evidence than in criminal cases.

Character evidence

The rule is that character evidence (good or bad) is almost always irrelevant except in order to attack the credibility of the witness generally.

Different considerations exist than in criminal cases. There is usually no danger of repercussions in civil cases, whereas in criminal cases the accused's character and record can be exposed.

A criminal record can be used in civil cases to undermine credibility where the conviction(s) are relevant to or suggestive of dishonesty, but again, no further.

The best evidence rule

As with criminal cases, the best evidence should be provided and secondary evidence where better evidence is available can be disallowed. This applies to real and documentary evidence.

In *Stewart v Glasgow Corporation* (1958), a corroded clothes pole had broken and killed a child. The pole itself was not produced in court and an expert gave his evidence based on an oral description by another expert who had examined the pole. His evidence did not corroborate the initial expert. Although no objection was made and the evidence was heard, pointed reference was made by the initial court and the appeal court to fact that pole was not produced.

An electrical fire was not produced in *McGowan v Belling & Co* (1953), a case arising out of injuries caused in a house fire, which was alleged to have started due to a faulty heater manufactured by the defenders. Experts sought to give evidence for the pursuer on the likely cause of the fire but this was based on an examination of a heater that was similar to the one in question. They had never seen the original heater, nor was it produced in court. The expert evidence was declared inadmissible by Lord Cowie in the Outer House.

Turning to documentary evidence, it has been made clear that where a document is fundamental to a claim, non production of the original can be fatal, unless a "no fault" explanation for the absence of the original can be provided.

In *Scottish and Universal Newspapers v Gherson's Trustees* (1987), certain financial records were not produced at all. This was fatal to the admissibility of oral evidence as to their content. The Inner House, in supporting the decision of the Outer House judge, held that the pursuers had failed to take "proper and elementary steps" to retain the documents, and that as the absence of the documents was therefore not due to an absence of fault on the part of the pursuers, the oral evidence was inadmissible. The court also indicated that in considering such issues, the extent of any prejudice that would result to the other party would be a factor. See also *Inverclyde DC v Carswell* (1987).

Overall, it seems that in the civil courts, a less relaxed view of secondary evidence is taken than in the criminal courts. There is some discussion in the main civil cases on the issue of prejudice, but while prejudice plays a key role in similar criminal cases, it holds less prominence in civil cases.

In the case of documentary evidence, the need to produce original documents can be overcome by a joint minute signed by both parties agreeing that a copy is a true copy of the original. Alternatively, the document can be duly authenticated as a true copy under s.6 of the Civil Evidence (Scotland) Act 1988 (but only where it is authenticated before the start of the proof—*McIlveny v Donald* (1995)). Finally, a declarator of the Court of Session proving the tenor of a lost document can be sought. This is a drastic course to adopt since a separate court action is needed, but is sometimes necessary, *e.g.* in the case of a lost will.

Irregularly obtained evidence

The way in which evidence is recovered takes up much more time and space in the rules of criminal evidence than in civil evidence. In Scotland, if evidence later relied on in a civil action is obtained legally, albeit in an "underhand" way, it will be admissible. The position on illegally obtained evidence is less certain. Many cases involve divorce actions and breaches of privacy.

Obtained irregularly but not illegally

The present position is that stated in the cases of *MacNeill v MacNeill* (1929) and *Watson v Watson* (1934). In *MacNeill*, a divorce action on the grounds of adultery, the husband had discovered a letter lying on the floor in the matrimonial home where it had fallen in the absence of a letter box. He went there during the period of separation. The letter was meant to be opened by his wife, who was not in the home when it was delivered and was addressed to her by her lover, using a pseudonym. The husband opened the letter, and saw that it bore evidence of an adulterous relationship between the author and his wife. It was held that the husband could rely on the terms of the letter in his divorce action since he had discovered its content by chance.

In *Watson,* another divorce action based on adultery, the husband had discovered in an open bureau in the home where he and his wife were residing, a torn up draft letter written by his wife to her lover, which was "addressed in passionate terms". It was held that this letter was admissible as having been discovered by chance and the fact that it was torn up and had not been sent was irrelevant.

Obtained illegally

As far as illegally obtained evidence is concerned, the position at present is uncertain. The most authoritative case on the issue is the Inner House decision of *Rattray v Rattray* (1897). In this case, (again a divorce action based on adultery) the husband sought to rely on a letter passing between his wife and her lover which he had stolen from the Post Office. By the time of the hearing of the divorce action, he had been convicted of the offence of theft of the letter and had served a short period in prison. In a

2–1 decision, the court allowed the evidence to be admitted on the basis that if it was relevant, the court should look at it however it was obtained.

In spite of this decision, there are indications that the Scottish courts dislike *Rattray*. So, *e.g.* in the case of *MacColl v MacColl* (1946), Lord Moncrieff followed *Rattray* with reluctance, but felt that he had to since it was an Inner House decision.

More recently, there seems to have been a move towards a more case by case test of fairness. In *Duke of Argyll v Duchess of Argyll (No.3)* (1963), yet another divorce case, the husband had obtained certain diaries written by his wife by breaking into his wife's home and stealing them. The diaries were admitted in evidence. However, in proposing the use of the test used by Lord Justice-General Cooper in the criminal case of *Lawrie v Muir* (1950), Lord Wheatley in the Outer House said this:

> "There is no absolute rule, it being a question of the particular circumstances of each case determining whether a particular piece of evidence should be admitted or not. Among the circumstances which may have to be taken into account are the nature of the evidence concerned, the purpose for which it is used in evidence, the manner in which it was obtained, whether its introduction is fair to the party from whom it has been illegally obtained and whether its admission will in fairness throw light on disputed facts and enable justice to be done."

More recently, in an immigration case, Lord Cameron (again in the Outer House) suggested that information obtained from an alleged illegal immigrant by immigration officials had been unfairly obtained as a caution had not been administered. Lord Cameron stated that the general test was one of fairness (*Oghonoghor v Secretary of State for the Home Department* (1995)). However, the driving force in this case was that the liberty of an individual was at stake, so although this is a civil case, it is arguably more akin to a criminal one in its nature.

It remains to be seen whether the *Rattray* decision will hold good in the future, but it seems unlikely. For the time being, it is the only Inner House authority in the area and therefore remains authoritative.

ECHR and privacy

The right to respect for privacy in Article 8 of the ECHR adds to the question of irregularly obtained evidence in civil cases. This Article was applied in *Martin v McGuiness* (2003). One of the questions in that case was the compatibility of the tactics of a private investigator employed to gather evidence to discredit a personal injury claim, with the right to privacy enshrined by Article 8. This particular investigator had approached the home of the pursuer and pretended to the pursuer's wife to be an old acquaintance of her husband. He persisted in his anxiety to see the pursuer when told by his wife that he was not at home. The pursuer heard of the visit when he returned and the view was quickly formed that this had been an attempt by a prospective burglar to prepare for a break in. An alarm was fitted and the pursuer and his wife continued to be anxious about a possible theft.

The investigator also set up a telephoto lens in an adjacent property and filmed the pursuer's movements while he was in the curtilage of his property. A question arose as to the admissibility of evidence of the observations of the investigator, as a result of his surveillance work. The line to be taken was that the pursuer had been exaggerating the effect of his injuries.

Lord Bonomy in the Outer House had no difficulty in holding that the actions of the investigator were in breach of Article 8(1). However, he held that the admissibility of evidence of such surveillance was saved by being "necessary in a democratic society" in terms of Article 8(2). The balance, according to Lord Bonomy, is between:

"...the interest of the pursuer in the security and integrity of his home as part of his right to respect for his private and family life and the competing interest of the defender in protecting his assets, and the interests of the wider community in protecting theirs..."

In this case, the scale was tipped in favour of the latter. No doubt, however, the intrusion in a future case might be more significant and the decision different.

Another relevant case, this time an English decision, is that of *Douglas v Hello! (No.6)* (2003). This case involved the question of who had the exclusive rights to publish the photographs of the wedding of celebrities Michael Douglas and Catherine Zeta-Jones. The court had to consider, when dealing with the Human Rights Act argument, the interaction between Article 8 and the freedom of expression right, covered by Article 10.

Hearsay Evidence

The position in Scotland is regulated by the Civil Evidence (Scotland) Act 1988. The important provisions of this act are:

"s.2 Admissibility of hearsay.
(1) In any civil proceedings—
(a) evidence shall not be excluded solely on the ground that it is hearsay;
(b) a statement made by a person otherwise than in the course of the proof shall be admissible as evidence of any matter contained in the statement of which direct oral evidence by that person would be admissible; and
(c) the court, or as the case may be the jury, if satisfied that any fact has been established by evidence in those proceedings, shall be entitled to find that fact proved by the evidence notwithstanding that the evidence is hearsay.
....."

s.9 Interpretation.

> In this Act, unless the context otherwise requires—
> ... 'statement' includes any representation (however made or expressed) of fact or opinion but does not include a statement in a precognition..."

Unlike in England, there are no rules of court to supplement these provisions and they stand alone. There are one or two matters arising out of these provisions that require to be discussed.

One point of general note is that whether the statement maker gives evidence of his own hearsay statement or not, the courts are willing to admit evidence of that statement (*F v Kennedy (No.2)* (1992)). In this case, a child witness did give evidence. However, the statement was not put to him. In *Sanderson v McManus* (1997), the child was not called to give evidence at all. In both cases the hearsay evidence was admitted.

The competency test

It appears at first glance that hearsay evidence, in terms of s.2 of the Act can only be led where the evidence, had it been led from the original source, would have come from a competent witness. We will come to the competency of witnesses in civil cases later. It was thought that the wording of s.2 was insisting that the original witness would have to qualify as a competent witness, had he been giving evidence in person (see the cases of *F v Kennedy (No.1)* (1992); *M v Kennedy* (1993); *L v L* (1996); *Sanderson v McManus* (1997). In all of these cases, the court proceeded on the basis that this interpretation of s.2 was correct. However, there were different approaches on when the question of when the competency test should be applied—date of statement or date of hearing? The crucial words here are "of which direct oral evidence by that person would be admissible" in s.2(1)(b), above.

In a landmark case before five judges, *T v T* (2000), the view was taken that s.2 did not embody a competence test at all. The Inner House in this case held that it was implicit in the statute that the maker of the statement would be a competent witness. The statute was referring to the possibility of inadmissibility of the statement for other reasons, *e.g.* due to the lawyer-client privilege (see later). Hence, s.2(1)(b) refers not to the competency of the witness but the admissibility of the statement. There is therefore no need in Scotland for hearsay evidence to come from a witness who was competent at the time the statement was made or who would have been competent at the date of the evidence. Such a person may have lacked competence on both dates (for example due to being too young to understand the difference between truth and lies), but the statement would still be admissible. Of course, the weight to be afforded to such statements will depend upon the circumstances of the case. One benefit of this interpretation is that hearsay statements from children can be used in cases where, *e.g.* the child is too distressed to be able to give oral evidence.

Precognitions

As will be seen from the definition of "statement" in the 1988 Act, it does not include a precognition. The term "precognition" is undefined by the Act, but case law makes it clear that it is an account taken from a witness and put into the words of the statement-taker—not the actual words of the witness. If an account is in the words of a witness, it is a statement. This distinction is crucial since a precognition is inadmissible while a statement is admissible.

The objection to the admissibility of a precognition (which also exists in criminal cases) as Lord Justice-Clerk Thomson put it in the criminal case of *Kerr v HMA* (1958), is that in such cases the account is "filtered through the mind of another". It is unlike a *verbatim* (word for word) account and is not completely reliable evidence of what was actually said. The distinction between the two has been argued in various cases in Scotland. It has been made clear in a number of these cases that it is only the precognition document itself that is inadmissible. In other words, evidence can be led from the precognoscer who may be asked what he or she recollects of what was *actually* said. This is not a breach of the rule against a precognition. (See Lord Clyde in *Cavanagh v BP Chemicals* (1995); Lord Morton of Shuna in *Anderson v Jas B Fraser & Co Ltd* (1992); affirmed by Lord Hardie in *Ellison v Inspirations East Ltd* (2003)). The position was put in this way by Lord Morton of Shuna in *Anderson*:

> "It appears to me that in civil proceedings the only reason for the exclusion of a precognition is that what is stated in the precognition is or may be coloured by the mind of the precognoscer who produces in the precognition an edited version of what the witness has said. This would exclude the actual document prepared by the precognoscer but would not exclude evidence of what the witness actually said to the precognoscer prior to the preparation of the document. I am of the opinion that the exception in the definition of 'statement' in the Civil Evidence (Scotland) Act excluding 'a statement in a precognition' means what is recorded in a document prepared by the precognoscer and does not exclude evidence of what the person said to the precognoscer in interview. On that basis Miss Neilson's evidence, for what it is worth, is admissible."

Having said this, it has been made clear by the courts that the account given by the precognoscer in such a situation is not likely to be regarded as a strong piece of evidence (see *Cavanagh*, where Lord Clyde commented upon the absence of an exact record of what the witness had said as being a weakening factor, also see *Anderson, per* Lord Morton).

Alternatively, the common law can be relied upon to seek admission of a precognition where the witness has, by the time of the hearing, died. This has been covered already in Part 3 and the cases cited there, namely *William Thyne (Plastics) Ltd v Stenhouse Reed Shaw (Scotland) Ltd* (1979); *Pirie v Geddes* (1973) and *Moffat v Hunter* (1974).

Statutory documentary evidence

Finally on admissibility in civil cases, evidence can be admissible as a result of complying with certain statutory provisions that essentially allow such evidence to be offered in the form of a statutory shortcut. The relevant provisions are ss.5–6 of the Civil Evidence (Scotland) Act 1988:

- s.5—a document which is certified as being part of business records will be taken to be so and no witness need speak to it;
- s.6—a document that is authenticated by the author as a true copy of the original will be treated as an original (however, a witness will be needed to speak to it, unless also certified in terms of s.5).

In connection with public records, under s.41 of the Registration of Births Deaths and Marriages (Scotland) Act 1965, an extract or abbreviated certificate of birth, death or marriage is self- proving.

WITNESSES

The same distinction applies here as in criminal cases—witnesses can be competent, and if so, may be compellable.

In civil cases, the following witnesses are treated in the same way as in criminal cases:

- Judges, prosecutors and defence solicitors
- Heads of state
- Diplomats and consular officials
- Bankers
- Insane witnesses
- Witnesses with communication problems

The following will now be dealt with in the context of civil cases:

- Spouses
- Previous attendees in court
- Vulnerable witnesses

Spouses

Section 3 of the Evidence (Scotland) Act 1853 provides that a spouse is competent in civil proceedings (except in cases under the marital communications privilege, dealt with below), however, there is no mention of compellability. Despite this, it is accepted that a spouse is competent and compellable, although there remains some doubt in consistorial cases. In consistorial cases, it could be that a spouse is not compellable (see *White v White* (1947); *Bird v Bird* (1931)). However, these authorities may not necessarily be followed—these cases involved cruelty, therefore they might not be followed in "no fault" divorce actions. In any other case, however, it is accepted that a spouse is a compellable witness.

Previous attendees in court

Section 3 of the Evidence (Scotland) Act 1840 regulates the issue in civil cases. The court can allow the evidence of any witness who has been present in the case at an earlier stage without the court's permission where there was no "culpable negligence or intent" and where no injustice results. In practice, however, where the opponent does not object, there is no need to use the section.

It is also worth noting that parties to a civil action have a right to be present throughout that action, even if they later give evidence (*Campbell v Cochrane* (1919)).

Vulnerable witnesses

The Vulnerable Witnesses (Scotland) Act 2004 applies in civil proceedings as well as criminal. However, on information presently available, most of the provisions will not come into force for civil cases until at least 2008.

We have already dealt with the competency test for child witnesses in Part 3 of this book. The competency test, as applied in the past (pre April 1, 2005) is as provided in that Part. The abolition of the competency test affects both criminal and civil cases equally (s.24 of the 2004 Act) and the comments on this in Part 3 apply equally to civil cases.

On measures for the taking of evidence, again, the 2004 Act provisions will apply in due course in civil cases, with the effect of the creation of three categories of vulnerable witness. These categories, as explained in Part 3 of this book on criminal cases, apply here.

Special measures in civil cases

There are no such measures that apply prior to the coming into force of the 2004 Act. The main ones are set out in Part 2 of the 2004 Act (s.18) and consist of the following:

- live TV link;
- screen;
- evidence on commission;
- the use of "supporters"

All of the same measures will be available as those in criminal cases. In addition, giving evidence in chief in the form of a prior statement will be available in civil cases when the 2004 Act comes fully into force (expected in 2008).

Also relevant, both before and after the application of the 2004 Act is the Lord Justice-General's Memorandum on Child Witnesses, July 1990, which holds relevance for both criminal and civil cases.

Cases under the Children (Scotland) Act 1995

For most civil cases, the special measures will not be in force until around 2008. However, from April 1, 2005 the measures in Part 2 of the Act are available in certain cases under the Children (Scotland) Act 1995, namely appeals under s.51(1) of the Act and applications under ss.68 and 85 of that Act.

PRESUMPTIONS

As discussed in Part 1, there are different types of presumptions. We will deal with some examples here. Presumptions play a more prominent role in civil than in criminal cases.

Irrebuttable of Law

Such presumptions are irrebuttable since they cannot be challenged, in other words if fact A is proved, conclusion B is inevitably reached by the courts. They are presumptions of law since they originate from statute or case law. Examples include:

- Capacity in the law of contract
- Previous convictions in defamation action
- Prescription of legal rights

Contractual capacity

Since 1991, a child over 16 is deemed to have the legal capacity to enter into a contract (subject to certain exceptions and conditions) under the Age of Legal Capacity (Scotland) Act 1991 s.1(1)(b).

Previous convictions in defamation action

Where an issue in a defamation action is whether the pursuer committed an offence, proof of a conviction is conclusive as to this issue (Law Reform (Miscellaneous Provisions) (Scotland) Act 1968, s.12).

Prescription

This is the legal device which allows for the creation or extinction of legal rights by the simple passage of time. The main source of the law in this area, the Prescription and Limitation (Scotland) Act 1973, provides for both "positive" and "negative" prescription:

- Positive—a recorded title to land followed by 10 years continuous possession will give a good, unchallengeable title under the Act, whether the original title was good or not.
- Negative—an obligation will prescribe (become unenforceable). A right to claim will be lost if a relevant claim is not made within certain time limits, *e.g.* five years for a debt action.

Rebuttable of law

These also arise from statutory provisions or case law, but are able to be challenged in any particular case and "disproved". The main examples of such presumptions in civil cases are:

- Presumption against donation
- Age of child bearing woman
- Presumption of continuance of life
- Presumption of death
- Presumption of legitimacy

Presumption against donation

Where A gives something to B, the courts will presume that A did not intend to gift it. This is based on the assumption that people do not normally give something away for no return. It only applies to moveable property, not heritable. However, where there is no alternative explanation for the handover, this absence in itself could provide sufficient rebuttal (as long as a donation is consistent with the facts). For an example of this—see *Grant's Trustees v MacDonald* (1939).

Age of child bearing woman

The maximum age of a child bearing woman is presumed to be 53 years old—*G's Trustees v G* (1936), applied in *Munro's Trustees v Monson* (1965). However, this could be rebutted easily in any particular case due to the possibility (as a result of the advancement of science) of a woman who is older than 53 giving birth (at the time of writing the oldest woman to have given birth is 66!).

Presumption of continuance of life

Life is presumed to continue, unless evidenced to the contrary until at least 80 years. However, there are two statutory exceptions, both of which we are about to turn to. While the general common law rule has been important in some cases (see, *e.g. Greig v Merchant Co of Edinburgh* (1921)), the statutory provisions (below) have removed much of the practical application of the presumption today.

Presumption of death

There are two statutory situations in which the common law presumption of continuation of life does not apply:

- a "common calamity" under the Succession (Scotland) Act 1964, s.31; and
- where a person is presumed to be dead under the Presumption of Death (Scotland) Act 1977.

Common calamity

Where two people die in circumstances suggesting they died simultaneously or where it is uncertain which survived the other, it will be presumed, under s.31 of the 1964 Act that they died in order of seniority. The eldest dies first, unless the two are husband and wife, in which case it is presumed that neither survived the other. This presumption was created by statute to avoid the kind of situation in *Drummond's Judicial Factor v HMA* (1944). It should be noted, however, that it only applies where it seems that the deaths were simultaneous or where uncertainty exists—see *Lamb v Lord Advocate* (1976).

1977 Act

This Act allows a person with an interest to apply to the court for a declarator of death in respect of a missing person. There must be either evidence of death or evidence to the effect that the person has not been known to be alive for *at least* seven years. The court will establish a date and once granted, the declarator is conclusive for all purposes including dissolution of marriage (even if the person later turns up) and for succession purposes.

Presumption of legitimacy

Section 5 of the Law Reform (Parent and Child) (Scotland) Act 1986 sets up two presumptions:

- a man is presumed to be the father of a child if he is married to the child's mother at any point during the pregnancy; and
- if this is not the case, he is still the presumed father if both he and the mother have acknowledged that he is and if he has been registered as such on the child's birth certificate.

These presumptions can be rebutted by proof on the balance of probabilities.

Rebuttable of Fact

These allow a fact to be presumed once a certain threshold of evidence has been adduced. The threshold will be met in some cases and not in others. They are therefore unlike presumptions of law where one applies the facts to the presumption. They are less certain because their application varies from case to case.

These presumptions arise from case law. In previous cases it will have been decided that the presumption should come into play.

Possession of moveable property

There is a presumption that the person in possession of moveable property is the owner. In order to rebut this presumption, the true owner would have to show (1) that he was once the owner, and (2) that the possessor could not have acquired ownership. He might seek, *e.g.* to show that the possessor is only holding the goods for the owner or that they are being held under a hire-purchase agreement. For this presumption in action, see *George Hopkinson v Napier & Sons* (1953), a case concerning ownership of hire purchase furniture; and *Pragnell v Lady Skiffington* (1984), a case involving separation of a married couple (the presumption did not apply in this case).

Res ipsa loquitur *('the thing speaks for itself')*

This presumption is applicable in a negligence case. In order for it to apply, there must be (1) an absence of direct evidence of the cause of the incident and (2) the cause of the incident must be within the exclusive management and control of the defender. The original case in which this presumption was expressed was *Scott v London and St Katherine Docks Co* (1865). In that case, a barrel had fallen from the window of a warehouse owned by the defendants, causing injury to the plaintiff. There was no evidence available as to how the barrel came to fall. The court held that negligence had been established due to the operation of this presumption. Erle CJ said this:

> "..where the thing is shown to be under the management of the defendant or his servants, and the accident is such as in the ordinary course of things does not happen if those who have the management use proper care, it affords reasonable evidence, in absence of an explanation by the defendants, that the accident arose from want of care."

This case was followed by the House of Lords in the Scottish case of *Devine v Colvilles Ltd* (1969), a case involving an injury caused by a violent explosion at a steelworks. The court held that the presumption applied, given that a violent explosion in a steelworks does not normally happen unless those managing the works were not doing so properly.

Other cases where the presumption has featured include *Inglis v LMS* (1941) (railway accident); and *Fleming v C&W West* (1976) (electrical explosion).

PRIVILEGE

Sometimes a witness or a party can refuse to provide documentation or refuse to answer a question in a witness box, even when ordered to do so. That individual can only do this if the information that would be provided in the document or evidence is privileged information.

There are four main cases in civil litigation in which information may be claimed to be privileged. Each will now be dealt with in turn.

Privilege against self-incrimination

If to answer a question under oath or produce a document would expose a witness to a real risk of criminal prosecution, the individual can refuse to answer the question or produce the document. Since the scope of this privilege in England is similar to that in Scotland (except in one situation, dealt with below), some relevant English cases will be referred to here.

This privilege can only be invoked where there is a *real possibility* of a *criminal* prosecution. If the information might expose the witness to a civil claim, it must be revealed. It has also been made clear that the information need not be a confession of a crime, but may simply reveal evidence of the individual's involvement in it (*Slaney* (1832)).

The court must assess the risk of prosecution. In order to do so, the court must know what the evidence would consist of in order to decide on what is, essentially, a question of law (whether the privilege exists, justifying a refusal to divulge). As Lord Stephen put it in *R v Cox & Railton* (1884): "the secret must be told in order [that the court may] see whether it ought to be kept."

Once it is aware of the content of the evidence, the court must decide whether there is a realistic prospect of a prosecution, not just whether one would be feasible (see the examples of *Blunt v Park Lane Hotel Ltd* (1942); *Rank Film Distributors Ltd v Video Information Centre* (1982)). If it so decides, the witness should then be given a warning indicating that he is not obliged to answer the question or produce the document on these grounds. However, if the chances of self-incrimination represent only a remote possibility, the judge will not issue the warning (*Singh v HMA* (2004)). The role of the agents involved in the case may be crucial here, since it is not uncommon for an agent to spot a potential problem and then object to a question and ask the judge to issue the warning.

The only difference between Scotland and England in relation to this privilege is that in England the privilege can be claimed where to produce the document or answer the question would "tend to expose" the spouse of that individual to a criminal prosecution (Civil Evidence Act 1968 s.14(1)). There is no such rule in Scotland as the privilege is not transferable in Scotland.

Other points about this privilege are:

- the witness must still be in danger of prosecution at the time, *e.g.* if there has been a not guilty finding or if a witness is called as an accomplice (dealt with in Part 3) or if the witness has pled guilty already, the privilege will be lost since there is no chance of self incrimination *as a result of* the answer or document production;

- it does not apply to answers which may incriminate a spouse of the witness (in England such a privilege exists) although, if the spouse is giving evidence during his or her spouse's trial, the matter may be covered by the matrimonial communications privilege (see below);
- with the exception of adultery (see below) the privilege cannot be claimed where the answer might lead to *civil* liability being established. The answer must implicate the witness in a crime.

Questions designed to elicit evidence of adultery are in a special category. The privilege is preserved for these questions despite adultery no longer being a crime (s.2 of the Evidence (Further Amendment) (Scotland) Act 1874). Where the admission comes in an affidavit as opposed to oral evidence, the privilege does not affect admissibility. In *Sinclair v Sinclair* (1986), there was no evidence of a warning being given to the witness that he was under no obligation to answer questions before the taking of an affidavit from him. Despite this, the affidavit was held to be admissible.

The privilege can be removed by statute where the wider public interest outweighs the protection of the individual, *e.g.* in the criminal example of s.172 of the Road Traffic Act 1988 and the case of *Brown v Stott* (2001) (discussed in Part 3). The same principle can apply in a civil case, *e.g.* under the Bankruptcy (Scotland) Act 1985, s.47(3), a person declared bankrupt must answer any question relating to *inter alia* his assets or his dealings with them when being examined by the Trustee, even if the answers might incriminate him (although the answers cannot be used in any later criminal prosecution).

Marital Communications Privilege

Section 3 of the Civil Evidence (Scotland) Act 1853 suggests that the spouse is neither competent nor compellable where the situation involves evidence of a communication between spouses. There is no definition of "communication" in the Act but it could be written or oral. Although there is no direct authority on this, it seems that the privilege ends with divorce (but not separation) and only applies to married couples. Someone else (other than either party to the marriage) can give evidence of the communication. In other words, the privilege only applies to prevent a spouse from giving evidence.

The rationale behind the privilege is the preservation of the sanctity of marriage.

Legal professional privilege—solicitor and client communications
The communications between a solicitor and his client, written or oral, do not require to be divulged in response to a court order for the production of documents, or in response to a question under oath. The idea behind this privilege is that a client is supposed to be able to consult a solicitor in confidence. This confidence would be undermined if the client was aware that the solicitor could be forced to betray that confidence by the courts. The privilege covers communications between a solicitor and an advocate and between an advocate and the client.

Again, some English case law is relevant here.

The requirement of a professional relationship
The communication must have been made during the existence of a professional relationship. Therefore, where the individual is communicating with a solicitor to see if he will act for him and the solicitor declines, anything said during the declination is not privileged—see the English case of *Minter v Priest* (1930). In Scotland, this point has arisen but was not decided (*HMA v Davie* (1881)), however, it is likely that the English approach will be followed when the issue does arise.

The privilege is permanent and does not come to an end after the solicitor-client relationship ends. This is clear from the decision in the House of Lords in *R. v Derby Magistrates Court Ex p. B* (1995) where the communications that were sought to be relied upon had occurred some 17 years previously and privilege was held to remain attached to them.

The absolute nature of the privilege
The absolute nature of the privilege has been made clear—see the extraordinary facts in the case of *R. v Derby Magistrates Court Ex p. B* (1995). There, the privilege was held to exist despite evidence of the communication between the client and his solicitor being sought by the accused in a murder case, and where it was hoped that evidence of the communication might bolster the accused's defence.

Communication must be for advice
The communication must be directly related to the giving of advice. If not, the privilege does not attach. In *R. v Manchester Crown Court Ex p. Rogers* (1999), the Crown in a criminal case sought to establish that the accused had visited his solicitor's office at a certain time on a certain day. The solicitor's note of the time of attendance was not privileged and had to be produced; it was not made in connection with legal advice.

Motive for seeking disclosure
Sometimes, the purpose of the disclosure attempt will lead to a decision that the privilege does not apply. For example, where the very question the court is inquiring into is whether or not the communication was made, the privilege flies off. This occurred in the case of *Anderson v Lord*

Elgin's Trustees (1859). There, the question was whether the pursuer had delayed in raising an action. To determine that question the court had to hear evidence on the communications between the pursuer and his client. The privilege was held not to apply.

Similarly, where the nature of the solicitor-client relationship is the very issue being probed by the court, the privilege will not apply. The question in the case of *Fraser v Malloch* (1895), was whether a relationship of solicitor-client had ever formed. The privilege did not apply to communications in that case.

Communications in furtherance of a crime

Where the client is attempting to use the solicitor-client communications privilege in a case where he is alleged to have been involved in a criminal act directly involving the solicitor, the privilege will not apply. It should be noted that the solicitor need not be complicit in the illegal act for this to happen, as long as he is somehow being used to further the crime, whether aware or not. In *Jones* (1846), the client forged a will and added it to a bundle of title deeds delivered to the solicitor in the hope that the will, in the client's favour, would be implemented. The client was not entitled to insist on his privilege in that case. In *Micosta SA v Shetland Islands Council* (1983), the privilege stayed in place on the basis that the solicitor was held not to have been directly involved in the act, while in *Kelly v Vannet* (2000), the solicitor was directly involved (although his involvement was purely innocent).

The crime need not be intended by the client himself in order for the privilege to be ignored. In the House of Lords case of *R. v Central Criminal Court Ex p. Francis* (1989), a relative of the client intended to use the premises being purchased for illegal activity. Although the illegal intent was not that of the client, the privilege could not be relied upon.

Communications, not observations

Finally, it seems that the privilege only covers communications, not observations made by the solicitor during contact with his client. As *Wilkinson* puts it:

> "A solicitor must refuse to say whether his client confessed to a crime but must answer if asked whether he came to him wearing blood-stained clothing".

This has not been tested in the courts, but not all commentators take the same view as *Wilkinson* (see, *e.g. Walker and Walker*, para.10.2.3).

The position is not clear if evidence of the communication comes from another source and is illegally obtained. However, if it is innocently obtained, it seems that it will be admissible—see *McLeish v Glasgow Bonding Co Ltd* (1965). See the section on irregularly obtained evidence generally.

Privilege protecting communications *post litem motam*

While litigation is under contemplation, any communications between a third party (not the client) and a solicitor are privileged. The communications must be made for the specific purpose of the contemplated litigation in order to be covered by the privilege. These communications are sometimes referred to as communications *post litem motam* ("after an action has been raised"). However the literal translation is not accurate since litigation need not have actually commenced for this privilege to apply, it needs only to be in contemplation. A communication *post litem motam* is one made when it is in the mind of a party that litigation may occur, in other words "after it is apparent that there is going to be a litigious contention" (*Admiralty v Aberdeen Steam Trawling and Fishing Co* (1909)). This privilege does not just apply to the solicitor-client relationship (which might be covered by the communications privilege anyway—see above), but to any communications between other parties. The rationale is to allow investigations without risk of disclosure of results to the other side (see *Johnstone v National Coal Board* (1968), per Lord President Clyde).

This privilege has particular application to communications between a solicitor and a potential expert witness, and would cover, *e.g.* a letter of instruction to a witness and the report prepared by the witness. The idea behind this privilege in such a situation is that the solicitor should be able to freely conduct investigations prior to litigation without fear that he will have to disclose perhaps an unfavourable report on his client's case to his opponent or the court.

It is important to note that litigation should be in contemplation at the time of the communication. In *Wheeler v Le Marchant* (1881), a surveyor's report made to the solicitor of the defendant had to be produced by the solicitor since at the time it was prepared, no litigation was in contemplation, even though one later ensued.

The privilege does not necessarily apply to a communication made with a mixed purpose, only one of which is a contemplated litigation. This situation arose in the House of Lords case of *Waugh v British Railways Board* (1980). There, the widow of a railway worker killed following a train collision brought an action of damages against her late husband's employers. An internal report had been prepared by the defendants for submission to the railway inspectorate. The plaintiff sought recovery of it. It was a valuable source of evidence since it contained witness statements and other technical material on the cause of the crash. The report was also explicitly stated to be for the defendants' solicitor. The House of Lords held the test to be whether the contemplated litigation was the "dominant purpose" of the preparation of the report. Where it was not, the privilege did not attach. Here, it could not be said that the dominant purpose was for passing to the solicitor, so the privilege did not attach and the document had to be disclosed. The document had other important purposes such as the safety of railways. The court was explicitly influenced by the consideration of the administration of justice in that such an important document should not be able to be kept secret.

One other leading case is *Hepburn v Scottish Power plc* (1997). This case concerned a house fire, the cause of which was suspected to be a short circuit in the electrical distribution board in the house. The defenders instructed engineers to investigate the cause of the fire. They visited the house with the consent of the householders and took away parts of the distribution board. A new board was then installed and a report was sent to the defenders by the engineers. In this case the Inner House held that the report, although prepared only a few days after the fire, had been prepared *post litem motam*. However, there was an exception to the rule that such documents are always irrecoverable. Where an examination involves the destruction or material alteration of the subject matter of the examination so that the party inspecting is in possession of information about the cause of an incident and the other party is not, thereby, in a position to acquire such knowledge, then the report will not be privileged. This exception applied in this case, and so disclosure of the report was ordered.

It is clear that factual reports do not attract the privilege, while reports concerning litigation do. The distinction was dealt with in *Marks and Spencer v British Gas Corporation (No.1)* (1983). This case is also authority for the fact that parts of a report might attract the privilege while other parts do not. In such a case, the parts that do not can be released, but only if these parts are severable (in the *Marks and Spencer* case, this was deemed not possible).

An exception
There is a major exception to the general rule. A communication by an employee witness to his employer shortly after an accident will not be privileged, even if litigation is in contemplation. This rule was confirmed by the Inner House in *Young v NCB* (1957). However, the report in that case was outwith the scope of the exception and fell within the terms of the ordinary rule so was, therefore, privileged. Lord Justice-Clerk Thomson made it clear that the scope of the exception is limited in the following ways: authorship of the report (it must be by an employee); character of the report (a spontaneous account of the incident); timing of the report (it should follow shortly on from the incident—in the *Young* case the report was communicated 6 months after the incident).

The application of this exception was confirmed by the Inner House in *More v Brown and Root Wimpey* (1983).

Communications in aid of settlement

Privilege also attaches to negotiation communications between parties and the agents of parties. The rationale for this privilege is clear—parties should feel free to try to negotiate claims without worrying that their correspondence will be relied upon later. Also, negotiations should be carried out frankly and without fear, to make the negotiation process more valuable. It is in everyone's interests, including the courts and the taxpayer's that negotiation of cases is encouraged. It should be noted that this privilege covers not only settlement negotiations by legal advisers, but by anyone, including the parties to the dispute themselves, or anyone else on their behalf.

There has arisen a practice among lawyers of marking correspondence as being sent on a "without prejudice" basis. This happens as a matter of course and many lawyers believe that by doing so, the entire contents of the letter are protected. This is not so. Those parts of the letter that involve settlement negotiations do attract the privilege, but where assertions of fact or unequivocal admissions are made, the attachment to the letter of the words "without prejudice" do not bestow upon those parts of the letter any privilege at all. In fact, those words are, in themselves, meaningless. The courts will consider whether the content of a letter is privileged, or whether parts of it are, whether the words "without prejudice" are attached or not. It has been said that the attachment of the words "without prejudice" to negotiating letters between parties is usual and desirable, but they are not definitive (see the comments of Lord Griffiths in *Rush and Tompkins Ltd v Greater London Council* (1989)). In Scotland, a similar position is adopted. It has been held that "without prejudice" correspondence cannot be referred to except with the consent of both parties (*Bell v Lothiansure Ltd* (1990)). However, this is not a blanket rule. In *Ware v Edinburgh District Council* (1976), the correspondence was considered to be confidential, but the following comment was made by the court:

> "The words 'without prejudice' inserted in correspondence may not cover with the cloak of confidentiality all portions of a particular letter which do not strictly relate to a proposed settlement...Nevertheless, they do cover actual negotiations and, in particular, negotiation figures for a settlement".

In *Daks Simpson Group plc v Kuiper* (1994), a question arose over whether the privilege attached to certain correspondence that was written "without prejudice" and that referred to an attached schedule of agreed secret commission payments. The letter indicated that the solicitor who had written it was "prepared to accept" certain figures. This was held by Lord Sutherland in the Outer House to represent a "clear admission rather than a negotiating proposal" and, as a result, the privilege did not attach to it.

In *Gordon v East Kilbride Development Corporation* (1995), a statement by an insurer contained in a letter to the effect that liability was not in dispute was held to be admissible as an unequivocal (unconditional) admission.

It is important to note that the privilege is not dependant upon the stage reached and litigation need not be shown to be in contemplation.

The negotiations privilege applies to oral as well as written communications. It can also apply to parts of a communication only (*Ware v Edinburgh District Council* (1976)).

Waiver of privilege

A party in possession of a privilege can waive his right to benefit from it. He may do so expressly or impliedly. In the latter situation, he may not intend to waive the privilege, but his actions may be taken as such. When a party in possession of a privilege wishes to refer to a part of a privileged document, or to part of a series of such documents, he will have to be very careful since he may be taken to have waived his privilege in connection with the whole document or series. The test is whether the document(s) is/are "severable". In *Great Atlantic Insurance Co v Home Insurance Co* (1981), two paragraphs from a memorandum were introduced into the pleadings by the plaintiffs. The entire memorandum would normally have attracted solicitor-client communications privilege. However, since the part of the memorandum that was not referred to was on the same subject, it was held that the plaintiff had waived privilege in connection with the whole document, not just the disclosed part. The solicitor-client communications privilege was held to be waived in *Wylie v Wylie* (1967), when the client tried to rely on part of a course of correspondence with his solicitors, but sought to exclude other related parts on the ground of privilege.

Further reading:

D. Auchie, *Hearsay Evidence and Human Rights* [2004] 72 S.L.G. 19.

A. Brown, *Corroboration in the Light of Smith v Lees* [1997] 65 S.L.G. 60.

J. Chalmers, *Distress as Corroboration of Mens Rea*, 2004 S.L.T. (Notes) 141.

S. Christie, *Vulnerable Witnesses (Scotland) Act 2004* [2004] 72 S.L.G. 75 (part of criminal update article).

A. Cleland, *Testament of Youth* (*T v T* decision), 2001 S.L.T. (Notes) 329.

A. Cleland, *The Tyranny of 'Testing the Evidence': The Need for Reform of Scots Law on Child Witnesses* (2002) 7 S.L.P.Q. 232.

Corroboration of Evidence in Scottish Criminal Law (Contributed), 1958 S.L.T. (Notes) 137.

F.P. Davidson, *Corroboration in Distress* (1997) 2 S.L.P.Q. 30.

T. Denning, *Presumptions and Burdens*, (1945) 61 L.Q.R. 379.

N. Downie, *Towards a Child Friendly Court I*, 2001 S.L.T. (Notes) 179.

P. Duff, *Towards a Unified Theory of "Similar Facts Evidence" in Scots Law: Relevance, Fairness and the Reinterpretation of Moorov*, 2002 J.R. 143.

P.W. Ferguson, *A Note on Accomplice Immunity*, 2003 S.L.T. (Notes) 79.

P.W. Ferguson, *Corroboration and Similar Fact Evidence*, 1996 S.L.T. (Notes) 339.

P.W. Ferguson, *Proof of innocence*, 2004 S.L.T. (Notes) 223 (human rights and the burden of proof).

P.W. Ferguson, *Reverse burdens of proof*, 2004 S.L.T. 133.

I.J. Gibson, *A Critical Analysis of the Relationship Between Evidence of a Confession and the Law of Corroboration in Scotland* [2000] 68 S.L.G. 198—Part 1; [2001] 69 S.L.G. 4—Part 2.

L. Gillespie, *Expert Evidence and Credibility*, 2005 S.L.T. (Notes) 53.

G.H. Gordon, *The Burden of Proof on the Accused*, 1968 S.L.T. (News) 29, 37.

G.W. Gordon, *The Admissibility of Prior Statements of Witnesses and the Accused in Criminal Trials* (1995–96) 1 S.L.P.Q. 352.

R. Johnston, *Ice Cream Verbals,* 2004 J.L.S.S. 22 (opinion evidence).

M. McCannell, *Corroboration in Criminal Cases*, 1996 S.L.T. (Notes) 347.

M. McCannell, *Mair v HM Advocate*, 1999 S.L.T. (Notes) 295 (corroboration and identification).

R. McMenamin, *Case for the defence*, 2005 J.L.S.S. 16 (vulnerable witnesses).

D. Ogg, *Towards a Child Friendly Court II*, 2001 S.L.T. (Notes) 181.

P. Ferguson, *Corroboration and Similar Fact Evidence*, 1996 S.L.T. (News) 339.

A. Poole, *Productions, Hearsay and the Best Evidence Rule*, 1998 S.L.T. (Notes) 211.

F.E. Raitt, *Credibility and the Limits of Expert Evidence in Scots Criminal Law*, 2003 J.R. 29.

E. Russell, *Case and Comment: Hearsay Evidence of Children: T v T—A Welcome Clarification of the Law*, 2002 J.R. 209.

Scottish Executive Justice Department briefing *Vulnerable Witnesses: Vital Voices*, 2005 J.L.S.S. 14.

D.H. Sheldon, *Children's Evidence and the New Hearsay Provisions*, 1997 S.L.T. (Notes) 1.

D.H. Sheldon, *Corroboration and Relevance* 1998 S.L.T. (Notes) 115.

D.H. Sheldon, *The Hearsay Rule Devoured (or Swallowing a Camel, Straining at a Gnat and Flogging a Dead Horse)*, 1995 J.R. 504.

D.H. Sheldon, *Hip Flasks and Burden,* 1993 S.L.T. (News) 33.

R. Shiels, *Corroboration by Distress* (1994) 39 J.L.S.S. 293.

W.A. Wilson, *The Logic of Corroboration* (1960) S.L.R. 101.

APPENDIX: SAMPLE EXAMINATION QUESTIONS AND ANSWER PLANS

There follows some sample examination questions and answers. Some of these are taken from coursework/seminar questions used with students at The Robert Gordon University taking the evidence module on the LL.B course. Others have been composed specifically for inclusion here. There is an attempt to cover several different likely examination question types, although past papers, where available, should always be consulted in preparing for an exam.

It should also be noted that the answers are "answer plans" and are not full answers as would be expected in an exam paper. They give a general indication of the material that should be covered. In particular, when a case is cited in an exam answer, and where the facts of the case are relevant, the facts as well as the decision of the court should be explained there.

Question 1
Outline the facts and decisions in the following cases:

(a) *Constantine Steamship Line v Imperial Smelting Corp Ltd (burden of proof in a civil case)*
(b) *Rhesa Shipping Co SA v Edmunds (The Popi M) (burden of proof and standard of proof in a civil case)*
(c) *Maguire v HMA (corroboration and DNA—criminal case)*
(d) *Barr v Vannet (reasonable cause to suspect—criminal case)*

Question 1—answer plan

Constantine Steamship Line v Imperial Smelting Corp Ltd
This case involved the destruction of a ship which was under a charter party. The defendants argued that the contract became frustrated due to the destruction of the ship by an explosion. The plaintiffs were suing under the contract for failure to load the vessel. The cause of the explosion was unclear. Normally, the defendants would bear the burden of proof of the cause of the explosion, and that the explosion qualified as a contractually frustrating event. The House of Lords held that it would be unduly onerous to require the defendants to prove an absence of fault on their part—the plaintiffs would bear the burden in this case of proving fault. This decision was reached on the basis that a party should not

normally require to prove a negative, so the burden of proof can be inverted in a suitable case to avoid this.

Rhesa Shipping Co SA v Edmunds (The *Popi M*)

In this case, the central dispute was over what had caused the vessel, *The Popi M*, to sink. The immediate cause was a hole in her hull, and the dispute was over how the hole had occurred. The plaintiffs argued that the vessel had struck a submerged submarine and that such a cause of sinking was a "peril of the sea" and so the loss was covered under the insurance contract. The defendants argued that the hole was due to the effects of wear and tear, and so was not covered by the terms of the policy. The trial judge found neither explanation convincing (describing the plaintiff's explanation as "extremely improbable") but awarded the case to the plaintiffs on the basis that the defendants had not come up with convincing evidence to counter the assertion of the involvement of a submarine. This decision was affirmed by the Court of Appeal. However, the House of Lords took a different view, and found for the defendants. They indicated that the trial judge is not obliged to accept *any* explanation for the loss put to him in evidence, he could reject them all. Where all are decided to be improbable, they must all be rejected on the balance of probabilities test. Where that happens, the plaintiff has failed to discharge the burden of proof on him, and so loses the case. This case demonstrates the use of the burden of proof to completely resolve a case as well as the operation of the standard of proof in a civil case.

Maguire v HMA

This case is an example of the general position that where DNA or a fingerprint of the accused is found at the scene of a crime, where the scene is not a readily accessible public place, there is sufficient evidence of the guilt of the accused, in the absence of an innocent explanation by him for his presence there. The accused had been convicted of robbery. The sole incriminating evidence against him was the presence of his DNA on a mask discarded by one of the robbers at the scene. The complainer gave a description of one of the robbers, consistent with that of the appellant, but when giving evidence later, he indicated that the robber concerned was not in court, nor was anyone resembling him. The mask concerned was a multicoloured woollen mask. It had been manufactured from the sleeve of a woollen jumper and there was a bloodstain on the mask containing a mixture of DNA from several persons, none of whom was the accused. The appellant argued that the no case to answer submission made at trial should have been upheld since the appellant could have come into contact with the mask innocently, particularly given its origin. The High Court refused the appeal and upheld the conviction, holding that there was a sufficiency of evidence in this case.

In reaching its decision, the court relied upon a line of cases indicating that if the perpetrator of a crime leaves something behind at the scene of a crime, which can be unquestionably associated and identified with the accused (for example a fingerprint, garment or tool) and where no innocent explanation is advanced for the presence of the material in question, there is sufficient evidence from which to infer the presence of the accused at the scene (*Hamilton v HMA* 1934 JC 1; *HMA v Rolley* 1945 JC 155). In these cases, the corroboration comes from the absence of an innocent explanation.

Some emphasis was placed by the court upon the "distinctive and recognisable pattern" of the mask. In other words, having been shown the mask (as the accused was in this case) it was hardly conceivable that he would not have recognised it is an item of clothing he had worn previously.

The general test was stated in this way by Lord Hamilton:

> "*Much will depend on the nature of the item on which the fingerprint or other identifying link was found and its association in time and place with the crime. The readiness with which the accused may innocently have come to be in contact with such an item may be such that, even in the absence of an explanation from him, no inference of sufficient association between him and the crime can legitimately be drawn.*"

Barr v Vannet

In this case there were various justifications relied upon by the Crown in their argument that the constables conducting the search under s.23 of the Misuse of Drugs Act 1971 had reasonable cause to suspect the accused of possessing illegal drugs: at the time the accused was walking near a house, situated miles away from his home, where illegal drug dealing was believed to occur; he was continually scanning the surroundings as he walked along the street; on being confronted and being told of the constables' suspicions, he immediately ran off; while doing so, he was seen to put something into his mouth and swallow it. The officers gave chase and caught the accused. When they searched him, he was found to be in possession of illegal drugs. It was held that even prior to approaching the accused, there existed reasonable grounds to suspect, but that in any event the test was whether at the time of detention and search such grounds existed, and by that time this was beyond doubt. This case is an example of the operation of the statutory test for authority for a search of reasonable cause to suspect, which must give rise to objective reasons to justify a search. If such objective reasons do not exist, the search is illegal and the fruits of the search will be declared inadmissible, unless the illegality can be excused.

Question 2

James, who is 14, is accused of assaulting his friend Tony. He is taken in by police for interview after Tony has reported the incident. Tony alleges

*he was punched on the face and kicked on the head by James, causing
injuries requiring hospital treatment.*

*James comes to the police station voluntarily, and as soon as he arrives
at the front desk, on giving his name, he breaks down in a fit of tears and
tells the front desk police officer that he carried out the crime.*

*He is then taken by another police officer, who is investigating the crime
(but who did not overhear the confession) to an interview room. James is
still visibly upset. The officer asks him what the problem is and he
confesses again. The officer notes down what he says and then cautions
him. James then says he wants his parents to come before he says
anything else. The police officer says that there is no need for that and
they should just continue the interview. James refuses and asks for a
lawyer to be present. The officer refuses again—there is no need, he has
already confessed and he wants to clear up the details.*

James, while still upset, provides a full and detailed confession.

(a) Is the initial confession at the front desk admissible?

*(b) What about the repetition of that confession to the second police
officer?*

*(c) If any details beyond a basic confession are revealed in the final
interview with the second police officer (after his refusal to allow both
lawyer and parent access) would these details be inadmissible? Why
might these details be important to the Crown?*

*(d) Would your answers to (a) and (b) be any different if James had
calmly asked to speak to a police officer at the desk and had broken down
and confessed in the interview room but before the interviewing police
officer had a chance to say anything to him?*

Question 2—answer plan

Model Answer

(a) It is admissible. James has attended voluntarily and he offers the
confession without prompting. This situation is even less stark than that
facing the accused in *Custerton v Westwater* where an incriminating
statement was issued in answer to a neutral but apparently loaded
question. The test in all cases is whether what has happened been fair
(Lord Justice-General Emslie in *Lord Advocate's Reference (No.1 of
1983)* following Lord Justice-General Clyde in *Brown v HMA* and
followed again in *Codona v HMA* in the opinion of the court, including
Lord Justice-General Hope) and there is no suggestion of unfairness here.

(b) This is a little trickier. One of the questions relates to the timing of the
caution. Much will depend on the information the second officer has. If
he has been told about the confession uttered at the desk, James should be
cautioned before he is asked what the problem is since suspicion will, by

now, have well and truly crystallised on him, taking the investigation to the second stage (the three stages as outlined in *Chalmers v HMA*) and he is certainly more than a "mild suspect" (*HMA v McPhee*). However, a caution is not always necessary even at stage 2 (*Pennycuick v Lees*). Having said that, in this case, there seems no reason for not issuing a caution, if the investigation is at stage 2, as there was in *Pennycuick*.

It is possible that the investigation is still at stage 1 when the initial account is given to the second officer. It is possible that James has simply been ushered through with no explanation given to that officer of the confession at the front desk. In that case, there is no need to deliver a caution, since the officer is simply interviewing a person for the first time, and will not be aware that he is even a suspect; for all he knows, James might be a potential innocent witness to a crime.

If a caution is deemed to have been necessary, the terms of the caution require to conform to the common law caution, and consist of the two elements of: (1) the right to remain silent; and (2) anything said might be used as evidence in court. Otherwise, the caution is inadequate and this might imperil the admissibility of the confession (*Tonge v HMA; HMA v Von*).

James' age is also an issue. The courts have indicated that the youth of a suspect can be a factor in considering the core issue of fairness (*LB v HMA*; *Hartley v HMA*; *Chalmers v HMA*; *HMA v Aiken*; *HMA v Rigg*) but it is only one factor. This would be a factor aside from the issue of the caution.

James is "visibly upset" at the time, and the physical and mental state of the suspect is another factor to consider in looking to the overall test of fairness (*HMA v Rigg; HMA v Aitken; Chalmers v HMA*). Again, this is one factor whatever the caution situation is.

(c) The refusal of access to parents of the suspect (at this point James has now been cautioned), is likely to weigh heavily against admissibility as is the refusal of access to a lawyer, particularly given the age and mental fragility of the suspect. There is no absolute right to the presence of a lawyer or anyone else during interview, but the ultimate question with a confession is, as ever: in all of the circumstances was what happened fair? Also, the fact that James is still upset when providing the full and detailed confession would weigh against admissibility. It is also arguable that the purpose of the interview is now to extract a detailed confession, perhaps one that would qualify as a special knowledge one. Where the purpose of an interview goes beyond investigation and onto the extraction of a confession, this can be relevant as a factor against admissibility (*Chalmers v HMA*; *Tonge v HMA*).

The detailed confession might be of importance to the Crown since it may contain special knowledge. A confession to a crime, no matter how clear, will not in itself be enough since it is from only one source and the confession needs to be corroborated. Corroboration may be found in the special (inside) knowledge exhibited by the suspect during his confession, as long as the only reasonable explanation for that knowledge is that the suspect is the perpetrator of the crime (*Woodland v Hamilton*).

In addition, there is evidence of an inducement of sorts offered by the interviewing officer. He suggests that there is no need for the presence of a parent and he advises that the interview should be continued. Also, he suggests, when a lawyer is requested, that this is not needed either, since the confession has been given and the details need to be cleared up. Either or both of these might, in the context of an interview with a young, vulnerable suspect be regarded as an inducement to continue with the interview. While this is stretching the idea of an inducement a little, even if these statements by the officer could only be regarded as encouragement to continue (as opposed to an outright inducement), this would be one factor to add to the mix in considering the overarching fairness test.

(d) Yes, since there would be no need for a caution before the confession was provided (as explained above, in the original scenario, one might have been necessary). However, all of the other factors would still be relevant: his age, mental state, denied requests for parents and lawyer, motive for further questioning, possible inducement or encouragement. In this situation, the detailed confession might be inadmissible, but the initial one to the interviewing police officer would not be.

Question 3

A collision occurred between two vehicles on a straight section of road. You represent the defender in the action raised by the pursuer who was injured as a result of the collision. Shortly before the collision, your client's car came onto the straight piece of road having just negotiated a sharp bend. The collision occurred just as the pursuer's car was straddling both carriageways in the course of performing a 3-point turn just after the bend. Your client's argument is that he did not drive negligently, because as he came round the corner at normal speed he braked as hard as he could but could not avoid the collision. Your client's position is that he stayed within the speed limit and on the correct side of the road at all times. He blames the pursuer for being partly on the wrong side of the road just around a sharp bend.

PC Plodd, a road traffic police officer of twenty years experience, is called by the pursuer to give evidence. He arrived on the scene just after the accident as a result of a call from a member of the public. He sees the cars in the accident position—they have not been moved. He carefully examines the accident scene and takes statements. While giving evidence, he is asked by the pursuer's lawyer whether he thinks your client should have been able to see his client's car round the bend if travelling at normal speed.

(a) Do you object to this question being answered? If so, on what basis?
(b) What kind of evidence do you think you might have been led instead of, or in addition to, that from PC Plodd?

Question 3—answer plan

(a) The question is probably objectionable, since it is designed to elicit opinion evidence from a lay witness. Generally only skilled witnesses are entitled to give opinion evidence. However, no minimum qualifications (or indeed any qualifications—*R v Silverlock*) are required in order to allow someone to be regarded as a skilled witness. There are two arguments that can be made in favour of admissibility. The first is that the witness is being asked to comment on something that he has observed—the layout of the road. A lay witness is entitled to comment on something he has seen, heard or sensed, but only where it would be reasonable for him to comment on such a matter. As someone who visited the scene, it might be possible to say that the officer is such a witness. However, this argument is unlikely to be accepted since the witness is being asked to comment not only on the layout at the scene, but also on the impact of that layout on the cause of the accident. This arguably goes beyond what a lay person would be reasonably able to comment on. The second approach is to seek to justify the question on the basis that the witness is a skilled witness. We are told that he is a road traffic policeman and that he has been so for 20 years. We would need to know more about his experience—how many accident scenes has he examined, for instance—but in theory it might be possible to argue that he is a skilled witness, even though he is not an expert witness. The case might become one that is comparable to the cases of *Hewart v Edinburgh Corporation; White v HM Advocate* and *Wilson v HM Advocate,* but particularly the *Hewart* case, which involved a policeman with inspection duties and experience. However, it is unlikely that this approach would be accepted since the courts would expect evidence of this kind to come from an expert.

(b) Evidence from an expert road traffic accident examiner would be advisable here. He would be able to carry out an examination of the scene and would be experienced and perhaps even qualified in this art. It is even possible that such an expert could carry out a reconstruction of the accident (perhaps using computer technology or models) since it is now beyond doubt that experimental evidence of this kind is admissible (*Campbell v HMA*).

Question 4

Acme Nail and Screw Co is suing Hardwood Joinery for the price of a delivery of nails. Hardwood is refusing to pay on the basis that the nails are sub-standard. They allege that Acme has a reputation for supplying shoddy goods, and they seek to call various witnesses who are customers of Acme who will testify to these general shoddy supplies. Some of these witnesses are customers who have been supplied with nails while others have been supplied with screws. Hardwood seeks to lead all of the other customers as witnesses to give evidence on the general nature of Acme as a disreputable supplier of shoddy goods and also in order to make its case more believable.

(a) Will any or all of the evidence from these other customers be admissible?

(b) The customers also claim that the managing director of Acme, Mr V Shady, made certain representations on the telephone to them about the quality of the goods sold by him, in order to induce them to become customers. These statements were made over a period of 4 years to ten customers. These statements turn out to be false, and complaints are made to the police by all ten customers. There is only one witness from each complainer to each conversation. This results in Mr Shady being prosecuted for ten charges of fraud, all on the same complaint. The prosecutor seeks to lead evidence from all ten customers as to the statements made. Could this evidence be sufficient for convictions on all 10 charges?

Question 4—answer plan

(a) The answer is, perhaps. Generally, in a civil case, the rules on collateral evidence are less strict than in a criminal case. As long as the evidence has a reasonably direct bearing on the issues at hand, it will be admissible (Lord Osborne in *Strathmore Group Ltd v Credit Lyonnais*). In the case of evidence of incidents from outwith the facts of the case in hand (collateral evidence) this may be admissible if it will shed some light on the issues (*W Alexander & Sons v Dundee Corporation; A v B*). The problem in this case is that the evidence might be seen as a general attack on the character of Acme as a shoddy supplier. On the other hand, if the nails supplied by the company are manufactured in the same way, using the same machines and the faults relied upon by each customer are the same, the evidence might pass the reasonably direct bearing test (see *Knutzen v Mauritzen*). In the case of the customers being supplied with screws, since the product is different, the defect might be different and this makes it less likely that the evidence would be admissible. However, even here the evidence might be of a similar manufacturing defect and so the evidence might be admissible. Insofar as the aim is to portray Acme as generally shoddy, the evidence will not be admissible since an attack on character will not be permitted and this would apply to the reputation of an organisation as much as it does to the character of an individual.

(b) The answer is, possibly. The prosecutor has a problem, since he has only one source of evidence as to the content of the crucial statement in each case. He needs corroboration on each charge. The way around this is to rely on the *Moorov* doctrine, which might allow mutual corroboration between each of the charges. Between any pair of charges grouped together by the prosecutor for the purposes of a *Moorov* argument, they must be connected by time, character or circumstance *and* there must be some underlying campaign or adventure linking the offences. Here, we do not have enough information to allow us to know whether the doctrine can be applied. We are told that the statements have been made over a period of 4 years. While time lapse is important in the application of *Moorov,* there is no maximum time limit beyond which it is inapplicable (various cases, but more recently *Dodds v HMA*). However, as a rule of thumb, a time lapse of over 3 years makes the likelihood of arguing successfully for the application of *Moorov* less. Here, 4 years is the time gap between the earliest and latest representation. The gaps between some of the pairs in between might be much less. Also highly relevant are the similarities between the content of the statements: do they relate to the same goods? are the statements very similar? are they made in similar circumstances? It is suggested that the representations were made in order to win custom so perhaps all ten complainers were not customers at the time of the representations, and this would count as a similarity connecting them. All of the circumstances will be relevant.

In answering this question, the facts of some of the *Moorov* case law should be quoted to illustrate an understanding of the different aspects of the doctrine.

Question 5
Consider the following statement:

The requirement that the facta probanda of any Scottish criminal charge requires to be corroborated is a burden the Scottish courts could do without; it causes an imbalance in weighing up of the rights of the accused with the proper administration of justice.

Do you agree or disagree with this statement? State reasons for your answer.

Question 5—answer plan
Here, the following should be included:

- Description of the rule requiring corroboration—affects only the *facta probanda* (explain what this is);
- Explain that corroborative evidence is evidence that supports or confirms the primary evidence (*Fox v HMA*); and that is consistent with the primary evidence (*Macdonald v Scott; Miller v HMA; TM v HMA*), not evidence that is neutral (*Gallagher v*

> *HMA; Gonshaw v PF Lochmaddy*) and not dishonesty (*Fisher v Guild; Brown v HMA*) or silence (*Robertson v Maxwell*);

- Discuss how the corroborative evidence does not need to be, in itself, convincing, and can be thin and contextual (*Armit v O'Donnell*) and can even involve the exhibition of an emotion (*Smith v Lees; McCrann v HMA; Fulton v HMA*);
- Outline the exceptions to the corroboration rule: special knowledge confessions (*Woodland v Hamilton; Wilson v HMA* (1987); *Gilmour v HMA; MacDonald v HMA*), partial corroboration (*Campbell v Vannet*), the *Moorov* doctrine (*Moorov v HMA*), the Howden rule (*Howden v HMA*), the circumstantial evidence exception (*Little v HMA; Norval v HMA*), the statutory exceptions (routine evidence; ss.281–283 of the 1995 Act) and the DNA/fingerprint exception (*HMA v Rolley; Langan v HMA; Maguire v HMA*).

Then, you will be ready to briefly answer the question. You should refer on one hand to the valuable protection the corroboration rule affords against the possibility of wrongful conviction, since evidence from more than one source is required. You could also refer to the fact that there are many exceptions to the rule and that it applies to scant corroborative evidence, leaving the rule severely weakened. You might also mention the argument that in many other jurisdictions, there is no blanket requirement for corroborative evidence and how, in a case where there is only one witness (one source) but who happens to be very convincing, there will be insufficient evidence to convict. At the end of the day, you might come to the view that the fact that the rule is weak, but is there, means that there is an adequate balance between protection of the accused and the proper functioning of the administration of justice.

INDEX